Speaking Parts

Atom Egoyan

Coach House Press, Toronto

Speaking Parts

Published with the assistance of the Canada
Council, the Ontario Arts Council, the
Department of Communications and the Ontario
Ministry of Culture and Communications.

Canadian Cataloguing in Publication Data
Egoyan, Atom
    Speaking parts

ISBN 0-88910-451-4
I. Title.
PN1997.S64 1993   791.43'72   C93-093424-5

For Arsinée, my sleeping muse

Contents

Speaking of Parts

Introduction by Ron Burnett

1. Image and Imagination

O imagination, you who have the power to impose yourself on our faculties and our wills, stealing us away from the outer world and carrying us off into an inner one, so that even if a thousand trumpets were to sound we would not hear them, what is the source of the visual messages which you receive, if they are not formed from sensations deposited in the memory?

Italo Calvino, 'Visibility'

In the opening sequence of *Speaking Parts* the camera slowly drifts left to right across the screen. The sequence of images is confusing. There is no immediate explanation for why they are there, no rationale for linking one shot to another. We see a cemetery with photographs of the dead on their tombstones and then a woman watching television. Her face is expressionless. The camera pans to the television, and then moves into the piano recital on the TV screen. It moves from the pianist to the face of a man in the audience. The image freezes and focuses on the man's empty look. He is gazing into a space beyond the screen. He seems preoccupied and inward-looking.

The man at the piano recital is Lance, one of three central characters in *Speaking Parts*. His 'look' that frames the opening of the film is also the look of Lisa, who is watching him on television. Together, their gazes reveal the delicate balance between inner and outer worlds. But their expressions provide no easy and accessible point of entry. Crucially, both Lance and Lisa are spectators. Their status as viewers opens up a whole series of questions about images, about the complexity of sign systems, about where images come from, and about the links between thought and sight, sensation and memory. Is Lance dreaming as he listens to the pianist? What is Lisa thinking about as she watches him on television? Why would a film open in a graveyard?

Lisa's eyes could well be my own as I stare at the images of the film.

Introduction

Or, I could be Lance, sharing my experience with an audience as I watch *Speaking Parts*. All of these elements make and re-make the activity of viewing for me. They suggest that images don't easily lend themselves to explanation, description or analysis. *Speaking Parts* uses television and video to examine the impact of images on society. It deploys these images knowing that they are fundamentally cryptic. This is one of the central ironies of the film. *Speaking Parts* tries to play the role of commentator, engaging in the kind of critical enterprise that might, in another historical period, have been pursued in more textually oriented media, such as novels or works of criticism.

From the opening shots of *Speaking Parts* we move to a stark, white video mausoleum, a viewing theatre where the dead can be revisited through images. The third major character in the film, Clara, stares at video images of a young man whose relationship to her is at first unclear. We later discover that he is her brother Clarence, and that he died donating a lung to Clara. But for the moment the image seems to have no origin, no history. Clara watches her brother's image to reappropriate her memory of him, to find some ground on which she can repossess what has been taken away from her.

As in the previous shots of other characters, Clara's face and look provide few clues to her thoughts. Instead, they point to a number of Atom Egoyan's preoccupations in *Speaking Parts*. Given that the activity of viewing is an act of sight, thought and meditation, how can the complexity of viewing be *represented*? The same question might be asked of dreaming. Can dreams be shown on the screen? Can the internal world of the dreamer be brought to life? What would the images look like?

Egoyan is concerned with the relationship between image and identity: his film proposes that images have transformed the personal and public spaces of its characters. It suggests there is no point of separation between image and identity, no 'ground zero' (as Jean-Luc Godard once called it) where reality and image can be posited as different from each other. As the opening shots of the film reveal, there seems to be no point of departure and no end point where this proliferation of images can be explained with the kind of depth for which Egoyan is searching. In other words, although the film seeks to explore how its characters grapple with their past, history is absent. The three characters in *Speaking Parts* try to find some order, some way of explaining, both to themselves and to each other, why images have become so important, and whether the result is a largely empty edifice of illusions and lost hopes.

This sense of fragmentation, bounded by questions of truth and morality, drives the narrative of the film forward. Although Egoyan remains faithful to the idea that a story must be told, he questions conventional strategies of storytelling through a dispersal of image and narrative. A distinction is carefully drawn between plot and the need for innovation in structure and aesthetic organization. At one level, *Speaking Parts* is organized like a labyrinth. Characters shift from emotion to emotion without clearly established motivations. They bump into the obstacles in their path. They seem content to wander from experience to experience. At another level — which might be described as superstructural — they share a desire to control self-image and to write their own stories.

Clara writes a film scenario in which her dead brother plays a major role. Lance auditions and wins the part of the brother. Lisa, in a scene which I will describe in greater detail below, uses the video camera to question herself about love, truth and morality. Yet, even as they end up creating parts for themselves, all three also lose control. Clara's scenario is taken over by the film's Producer, who is not sensitive to the issues that she is trying to raise. Lance discovers that he is really a surrogate for Clara's brother, and that Clara is using the scenario to resurrect — if not reproduce — the love that has been taken from her, and to assuage the guilt that she feels over her brother's death. Lisa's experiment with video fails because she understands neither the medium nor the effects it has on the characters she interviews.

As soon as a character in the film experiences an image or an emotion over which he thinks he has some control, he loses something. This is most fully exemplified in the scene in which Lance pulls some roses out of a clothes dryer. The roses are a gift from Lisa, who is trying to display her love to Lance, trying to provoke him into understanding her feelings. But Lance cannot comprehend Lisa's gesture, just as she cannot really understand Lance or recognize that the roses will have no impact. Neither is able to work successfully with these symbols; it's as if for them *all* symbolic meanings have been disconnected from their roots. Normal codifications have disappeared, and what remains unclear throughout the film is whether meaning can ever be recovered despite these losses. This is where the labyrinth seems to have no exit, the mirrors and windows no purpose, other than to point to their own existence.

In *Speaking Parts* images create a world in which the real is just one element among many others. Images can refer to each other, can be an end in themselves, and can evade conventional restrictions of time and space. Thus the dead can reappear on video or in a photograph, and the irony is that they are of course *not* there. The photographs on a tombstone refer to what? To a memory? To the young face of an old man? To the middle-aged look of someone who has now become nothing? Their timeless quality seems to banish death or at least suggest some measure of control over absence; but this may be the greatest illusion of all.

Lisa wants Lance to love her, but in this case desire doesn't produce a result. Lisa satisfies her need for Lance by watching him on video in much the same way as Clara soothes her guilt over Clarence's death by repeatedly viewing him on tape. The image can be seen but it cannot be touched or caressed. In a sense, both Lisa and Clara possess the men they love, but they are only able to do so within the world of fantasy made available to them by the television screen. This is a world in which memories take on a form outside of the imaginary, where dreams come to life, where the swirling contradictions of thought and internal image can be given some coherence, can be linked one to the other.

The word 'image' refers as much to the pictorial as it does to something far more internal, to self-image, to images of self. It is not surprising that Lisa and Clara should seek to validate both their identities and their love through television and video: in so doing they demonstrate that television plays a central role in our culture, and in the home. The home becomes a generator of images, a place for the production of fantasy. Rather than being a device through which shows, ideas, news broadcasts and other images are received, television becomes one of many available tools that can be used to sustain daily life by sustaining the creation of images of self and other.

Lisa's love turns into obsession because she cannot see herself outside of the image that she has created of Lance, outside of the love that video has made possible. Her love is sustained by her narcissism and by her desire to capture Lance, to capture her imaginary boyfriend *as image*. Many of Lisa's key scenes take place in the Cloud Nine video store where she meets the clerk Eddy. Lisa goes there to rent videotapes of films in which Lance has played bit parts. She is also fascinated by Eddy's work videotaping weddings and parties, and other 'usual and not so usual' events. Eddy shows Lisa his video editing booth, where they view a wedding tape in which the father of the bride is brought to tears. When Lisa asks Eddy how he encouraged the sentimentality of the father Eddy says, 'You just got to know what buttons to push.'

For reasons which are at first unclear, Lisa wants to help Eddy shoot his videotapes. She follows him to a party and ends up wandering through a landscape of debauchery, the 'raw' material for soft-core pornography, heterosexual and homosexual love. Lisa questions why Eddy would be videotaping something that seems so irrelevant to her own concerns. Another video-sex scene and a second party sequence provide answers to her question.

In the next video-sex scene (intercut with the debauched party sequence), Lance and Clara masturbate while watching each other on large video screens. They are excited primarily by the manner in which they have become images one to the other. Masturbation is the only way in which they can express their attraction, and in order to experience each other the lovers have to *disembody* themselves. They get excited by the act of seeing each other as images, and transfer that excitement to their bodies. Since Lance cannot touch the image, he must look at it and touch his own body. This metaphor of the body in relation to the image, the body taking the image into itself and defining its sexuality in terms of the image, puts into question the very nature of the body itself. Where are the boundaries? We see Lance in the same way that he sees Clara: on-screen instead of in the flesh. This doubling makes the act of masturbation possible, makes the act of masturbation an act of viewing, transforms the body into a fulcrum for sight. Lance's body can only become a locus of pleasure if he keeps his eyes open. Egoyan has Lance masturbate in a detached and cool manner, like someone who has practiced the art and for whom the pleasure of self-love is the defining feature of love itself. We realize that both 'lovers' are faking their orgasms because they are actually actors, 'speaking' and playing their parts.

At no point then has anything really happened. Throughout this sequence, the fake masturbation becomes a metaphor for the simultaneous power and emptiness of images, the power to eroticize the body and the power to strip the body of meaning. A simple juxtaposition of a debauched party and masturbation evolves into a meditation on narcissism and voyeurism. The film asks why and how an image can be sexually exciting. The question is not so much whether these images should be suppressed. Rather, to what degree have image and sexuality become interdependent?

At the second party, Lisa videotapes Ronnie and Trish, newlyweds celebrating their marriage. After a moment, Lisa asks the groom to leave so that she can question Trish in private. Quickly and without any preparation, Lisa asks questions of the bride that she would normally ask of herself. This sudden intimacy breaks the conventional distance of the camera from its subject and raises an awkward question about the purpose

Introduction

of the wedding video. The interview was intended to be a record of the marriage, and like a series of photographs it was meant to highlight the positive nature of the event.

Lisa questions the bride: 'What do you see in Ronnie? When you look at him, what are you looking at? Have there been times when it didn't seem so … certain?' 'No,' answers Trish. 'I mean, these things are pretty delicate, aren't they?' Lisa asks. 'There's no telling what could happen. One of you begins to have second thoughts and — the whole thing can crumble away.' Lisa continues: 'I mean, love is about … feeling someone else feeling you, right? But sometimes … they may not act that way. In your case, it's the other way around. He says that he loves you, which is great, but I'm not sure if that matters. The question is, "Do you feel him feeling you the way you feel yourself?"' 'Why should I even think about it?' asks Trish. Lisa responds: 'Because years from now, when you look back at this tape, your answer might be really … interesting.'

Lisa is clearly not following the script — not saying what one should or even must, given the circumstances and the context. She introduces ambiguity into the event as well as the discourse upon which it is dependent. In so doing she disrupts both the interview and the party: Trish runs off in tears. How do you feel someone feeling you? And why ask that question for a videotaped memory of the marriage? Of course, Lisa is really asking herself this question. She is wondering whether or not she can 'see' Lance, and exploring her part in a relationship defined through images, a relationship in which the question has always been, 'What are you (we) feeling?' Trish and Ronnie's marriage is constructed by the film as a fairy tale; precisely the kind of fable that appears so often on the theatre screen, exactly the idealization that Lisa desires but cannot achieve.

The clash between Trish and Lisa is based in their differing approaches to identity. Trish believes in the process and in the ritual. Lisa does not trust herself enough to trust marriage, let alone love. At the heart of this scene is the almost therapeutic intent of the interview; Lisa thinks she can find answers with the aid of the video camera. She doesn't anticipate or understand Trish's response, and the result is a violent scene in which Lisa is thrown out of the party. Lisa's attempt to create a 'living' document that will serve as an historical reference predictably fails because, as *Speaking Parts* suggests, images generate idealizations that often have little to do with historical truth. Trish does not want to strip away her feelings before the camera because, if she does, an otherwise depersonalized process will become visibly personal and, potentially, public. Lisa doesn't understand that what is at stake is the way *others* will see Trish. The foundation of the bride's identity will be removed, and that is far more dangerous to the marriage than any feelings of doubt which Trish may harbour.

The marriage anticipates the images that will record it. It is, like a theatrical event, designed to *be* an image, to be played out as image. Lisa's transgression upsets the scenario of harmony and perfection, and also unveils the dependence of the event on the video that is to be made of it. At the same time, it is not as if Lisa understands what she has done. The violence puzzles her because, although she was on the other side of the camera and therefore in control, she acted as if the camera wasn't there. She does not realize that any negation of the camera's presence is a negation of the event. Another way of thinking about this is to anticipate what would happen if a marriage photograph of the bridegroom or the bride were taken when either or both of them frowned. Festive events require a smile in order to legitimate the photographic record. Without that overt expression of happiness, wouldn't the event itself seem tainted? So why does Lisa negate the control that the camera offers her? Why not make Trish comfortable and slowly integrate her into a scenario that would have encouraged the revelations that Lisa wanted? Could it be that Lisa's narcissism extends to Trish and that she sees herself as Trish? It is as if Lisa is talking to herself in a mirror: as if she does not understand the extent to which video creates the events it pictures. For her, video is a transparent entry point into the truth as she *desires* it. Her interview is a failure because she cannot cope with the truth as others see it.

2. Language and Sexuality

Much of the action in the film takes place in a hotel. Lisa and Lance work in the housekeeping department, though Lance also works as a male prostitute and a part-time actor. Hotels are not only about transience. They also represent the ironies of tourism: a home that is not one, temporary luxury, a retreat from the everyday that costs a great deal and that requires a complex infrastructure if it is to be maintained. While Lisa washes the clothes and sheets and then makes the beds, Lance vacuums bedrooms and cleans bathrooms. These perfunctory activities which they perform in a robot-like fashion are rarely interrupted by the

Introduction   comings and goings of guests. Hotels are also about loneliness: empty rooms devoid of memories, beds slept in by hundreds of people, the illusion of privacy. For Lisa and Lance the hotel is a state of mind. Here desires circulate through the fissures of an environment in which people make only superficial contact with each other.

In the hotel Lance is pictured as bisexual and sexually irresistible because he *looks* so female. As a result he is both a threat and a source of comfort. This is the allure of the prostitute and, the film suggests, of the soft-core pornography that dominates video stores. Others share what seems to be a private fantasy and/or they embody it. The prostitute is the body upon which those fantasies can be played out. But of course it is all temporary, and the prostitute is inevitably playing a role, catering to the *other* while all the while revealing the desire to be an empty hole that anyone can enter as long as he or she has the money. One of the crucial moments in the film comes when, having recognized that Lance's love is merely a role he is playing in the fictional universe of the hotel, one of his clients commits suicide. Lance's reaction to that death is the equivalent of a shrug. He reaches the point where his personality flattens out. He ceases to have an ethical framework within which he can judge the impact of events upon him.

The combination of the apparent meaninglessness of her job and Lance's calculated disregard for her provokes Lisa to turn to the image of Lance as a substitute for relating to him as a person. She watches and re-watches the bit parts he plays in what are clearly inconsequential films, and fantasizes a relationship that doesn't exist. Her viewing takes place in a room furnished only with a television and a videotape recorder. This room represents Lisa's mental space, one that she has to fill with something 'outside', with the image. But the image provides her with no points of departure, let alone possible avenues of escape. And it is this sense of enclosure, of being enclosed, that both links and differentiates her from Lance. His folly is to believe that the enclosure can be broken, that people are greater than their images, that the actor can transcend the limitations of his role. He cannot recognize how his identity is bound up with his image, how the bit parts he plays have slowly translated themselves into his daily life as the motif for his own existence.

If Lance is to survive, he must cater to the image that *others* have of him. At the same time he remains desperately unsure of his own identity. When Lisa propositions Lance in the employees' cafeteria she is observed by the hotel Housekeeper. Summoning Lisa to her office, the Housekeeper explains that she sees the hotel and its workers as a family which she guides and surveys. She makes it clear that Lance is a favourite child and Lisa is not. This construction of a perverse familial context full of power relations not appropriate in the work context also highlights the sexual paradoxes that develop through the process of surveillance: every activity in the hotel is observed and observable. The lack of privacy transforms the hotel into a playground for voyeurism in which everybody must play a specific part to satisfy the exigencies of the image and of viewing. It is as if, somewhat like a film, sex follows a script, has already been spoken, already been written, read and experienced.

This sequence opens up another set of questions. Clara relates to her brother as if he is a long-lost lover. The implication throughout the film is that her love for him was close to incestuous. Consequently, Lance becomes more than just a surrogate. Clara sets Lance up as an imaginary vehicle and attempts to fulfil a fantasy with Lance that she could not fulfil with her brother. The Producer's attempts to rewrite her script threaten Clara's fantasy. She does not understand that films are created through a process of negotiation between an industrial context and creative artists, and that the final product never looks like the original proposal or scenario. And she is incapable of incorporating the Producer's changes into her conception of the film and into her fantasy. Her life was shattered by the death of her brother. She is riddled with guilt and depression. The story she wrote for the screen is not only a way of purging that guilt, but also a means of bringing her brother to life, albeit in fictional form. Throughout the film, Clara is seen gazing at the image of her brother in the video mausoleum. Just like Lisa and Lance, she cannot separate the image from memory and so conflates them. What is at stake in Clara's script is the sacredness of memories that are filled with ambiguous feelings and saturated with the guilt of incestuous love.

These characters do not understand that images take the sacred and drain it of significance. For example, as Lance gets caught up in the machinery of the film industry, in the false ego-building of the Producer and the image others have of him, the process overwhelms the already confused image that he has of himself. When Lance immerses himself in his starring role he becomes an opportunist, and in so doing he loses contact with a moral centre, with a sense of what is important and what is not.

Clara's brother gave her his lung, the breath of life. The metaphor of the transplant is a fascinating one. Bodies — whether alive or dead — are interchangeable. Bodies are like tourists travelling from one location to another: homeless, embroiled in the surface of events, disconnected,

Introduction

reconnected, caught up in a constant flow between various levels, from one hotel room to another, from one city to another. The body has inscribed upon it all the various characteristics of the life that it has led. But these are also hidden from view, often as inaccessible to the individual subject as they are to the outside observer. So it is with Lance, who recognizes the effects of the prostitution upon him but cannot articulate its impact, who lives in a world where he cannot explain the ambiguities of his own feelings either with respect to himself or in relation to others. He is usually silent, and when he does speak he hesitates. Often he is so inward-looking, so distant, that Lisa's love for him seems unjustified.

Like bodies, images are interchangeable. Their meaning is always arbitrary. For Egoyan the image is a thing that substitutes absence for presence; there can be no co-existence between the two. The image merely sits in waiting — as do all video screens, whether on or off — sits and waits for the loss, the inevitable loss of meaning that is the motor force for the continued production of images and for the fabrication of personal identity.

The video or film camera has become more than a mediator between reality and the image: it is now a necessary part of both. And this is where the notion of speech comes in, for it is clear that in *Speaking Parts* speech as such has ceased to be valued or understood in isolation from the image which it is inevitably preparing itself for. The significance of what is spoken is constantly bracketed by the way the image will interpret, or has interpreted, what is said. The link between the image and its referents has been broken.

The autonomy of its processes is fundamental to the operation of the image; it becomes an object that somehow transcends its progenitors. This elimination of subjectivity lies at the heart of Egoyan's film, at the heart of a dilemma about the meaning of language and sexuality in an age in which the spoken and written word have been stripped of the consensus that normally guides their use. The film proposes that there has ceased to be a community of people that understand each other along conventional lines. Egoyan suggests that any over-investment in the image needs to be problematized if only to examine the image's capacity to simultaneously entice and undermine, to provide meaning and pull it away. What *does* happen when a video image, like some floating and ethereal essence, substitutes itself for a dead loved one? What does it mean to see a dead relative 'preserved' within the frame of a television set, neither able to reach out to the living nor to die and disappear? The video mausoleum is like a living archive. It is a world in which the body is caught by the camcorder and will never age. What an enticement! Yet, as Lisa discovers, while the video screen can replay anything and can be talked *to*, it cannot allow for the unpredictability of human interaction and human communication. It cannot, in other words, be anything more than a screen.

❖

3. Rites of Passage

I was told this by Rosa Maria Mateo, one of Spain's most popular television entertainers. A woman had written her a letter from some remote village asking her please to tell her the truth: 'When I look at you, do you look at me?' Rosa Maria told me this and said she didn't know how to respond.

Eduardo Galeano, The Book of Embraces

Clara stares at the video images of her dead brother, and it is as if he has come alive again. Yet, like a photograph on a tombstone, these images — played over and over in an unalterable sequence — are a reminder of all that is absent. Clarence's smile and walk remain frozen in time. His gestures become a ghostly reminder of death rather than a release from its effects. Clara is put in a position of grieving permanently rather than going beyond what her brother's death has done to her. Does she die a little bit each time she watches his video? In a sense, the video mausoleum is a metaphor for the narrative of the film: it is a room with many lives, all fragmented into loops, each replaying anxieties that can never be connected. Nothing can be shared in that room; its tomb-like silence is a reflection of Clara's bind. The power to control the image is a dangerous fantasy of viewing, yet the fantasy is a necessary one without which the act of viewing would be impossible.

Through the talk-show format Egoyan confronts the difficult relationship our culture has with the images it depends on. Talk shows are a window into the psyche of television. Guests confess to all sorts of ills, crimes they have committed or might commit. They are egged on by Donahue or Oprah or Sally Jessy Raphael to confess to a public that believes it has become a witness to the most intimate feelings of the people on-screen. The self is unveiled warts and all. Guests cry and scream at each other, taunt and are taunted by the audience. The aim is to get at a truth that otherwise will not be available. Inevitably the shows

Introduction

are orchestrated along the lines of a narrative and become fictional ex-orcisms of the way in which our culture relates to morality, to its own ethical underpinnings. Egoyan recognizes the centrality of the talk show and uses it as the focal point for the climax of *Speaking Parts*.

The talk-show host is both the Producer of Clara's film and the man who hired Lance to play Clara's brother. He is the man who seems ready to sacrifice Clara's intentions in order to meet the industrial exi-gencies of profit and the bottom line. The dissonance here is beautifully crafted; in playing all of these roles, the Producer becomes the evil other to nearly every character in the film.

In the opening of the talk-show sequence, the Producer addresses the audience: 'Now, what I want you to do is pretend that this is a real show. As if it were being broadcast live, and you are actual participants. Now, the topic of the show is organ transplants, and this is a life-and-death issue. Obviously, I need the tension level here to be quite high.' The sequence begins with the Producer's survey of the various elements being deployed to create the talk-show scene: actors playing doctors and the families of people in need of transplant operations; more actors in the audience; Ronnie as the dying David in a live feed from his hos-pital room; Lance, planted in the audience, waiting to announce that he will donate his lung to his brother. But then the talk show shifts into high gear and the Producer disappears into his role as TV host, in-forming people who have just tuned in that 'David is a young man des-perately in need of an organ transplant.' Intercut with this sequence are images of Lisa in the hotel, fiddling with a camera that seems to be part of a surreal surveillance system, and of Clara, doubled over on her bench in the video mausoleum.

Once Lance plays his part and announces that he will donate his lung to his dying brother, the montage intensifies. The live-feed image shifts, and Lance sees himself in the bed. Behind him in the studio Clara rises and puts a gun to her head. Lisa is suddenly a nurse and she bends over to kiss Lance in his hospital bed. The editing increases in pace until everyone's identity is blurred, and the lines of demarcation between screen, studio, Lance, Lisa and Clara are completely dissolved. Fictional and real elements pile upon each other until Lance finally screams 'No!' in a desperate attempt to break the relay of metaphors and prevent Clara from shooting herself. The screen dissolves into snow, and we are sud-denly back in Lisa's flat where Lance sits in a bare room. Lisa comes in and they silently embrace and seem to be reconciled. The television in the room is on.

The complexity of the talk-show sequence brings the artistry of *Speaking Parts* to a climax. Testimonials form the core of talk shows and bear witness to the extraordinary way in which 'life' and artifice become transparent, one to the other. Since the guests on a talk show are ordinary people the presumption is that what they say is true. They address a host, a live audience and a television audience with this truth as the force behind their words. (They are not meant to be acting.) They are witnesses to their own lives and invite others to join them in identifying with the revelations. In the scene described above everything is in place for the process to begin, but it is short-circuited, stillborn. In order for Lance to overcome the horror of Clara's possible suicide, the perverse show-biz re-enactment of Clara's own lung disease, the Producer's conflation of real life and cinematic artifice for the purposes of profit, and his own realization that he has been playing a role for others throughout his life, he must destroy the image and regain his body and self through Lisa.

But this sequence reveals that the use of the image as the foundation for human discourse provides a fragile framework for the construction of truth. The entire film plays in an ambiguous fashion with this question of speech, artifice and truth and, more particularly, with the rather perplexing problem of the actor's relationship to what *is said* in performance. There is obviously a large gap between the actor and acting, that is, between the star and the characters he plays. After all, it would be difficult for an actor to move from role to role if he were not able to shift his identity in a substantial way. But what if those shifts together merge into a composite image, a composite identity? How do we gain access to the differences between an actor and the life that he leads? How does the actor himself gain access to his own identity? It seems that we accomplish this in part through the media, that is, through images. So there is a double irony here, a classic case of doubling: in the media the real life of the actor is as much an image as the characters he ends up playing. It is all a matter of degree, of how the part relates to the whole, of whether the actor can or should transcend the limitations of the roles that he is always playing. This idea that the image is always double, never singular, also has an effect on the way we respond to images. It suggests that the pleasure of viewing is as much bound up with artifice as is the film itself, and that the spectator is also speaking a part, playing a role.

Although Lance finally realizes that he must break the circuit of roles into which he has willingly entered, the film concludes with the same

Introduction

binds that have governed it from the start. The 'testimony' of an actor is constructed according to the exigencies of a script. Somewhere in between script and real life, suggests Egoyan, there must be a space in which truth operates outside of the cultural and institutional constraints that are conventionally applied to human actions and language through image processes. The 'parts' that are spoken must connect to an ethical centre, must be governed by recognizable boundaries. At the end of the film, Egoyan proposes that it is the physical contact between two human beings that will transform the role of the image and generate another space within which different questions of identity can be worked out. Lance and Lisa discover their need for each other. The image of their touching transmits the intensity of their feelings.

Identity, be it national or personal, cannot be divorced from images. At this rather tenuous and fragile stage of our history, it may be necessary to discover a new way of using images instead of creating more contexts in which they use us. Egoyan's film is a proclamation that this can be done. The film ends, the show ends, the characters leave, but somehow the images never do. The circularity of image–viewer–image continues. Lisa and Lance are in each other's arms. The television set in her room is on: it is a mirror in which Lisa and Lance are trapped, a fairy tale with no ending, a loop that repeats itself interminably. Our innocence has been taken away forever, but more often than not we are surprised at the loss.

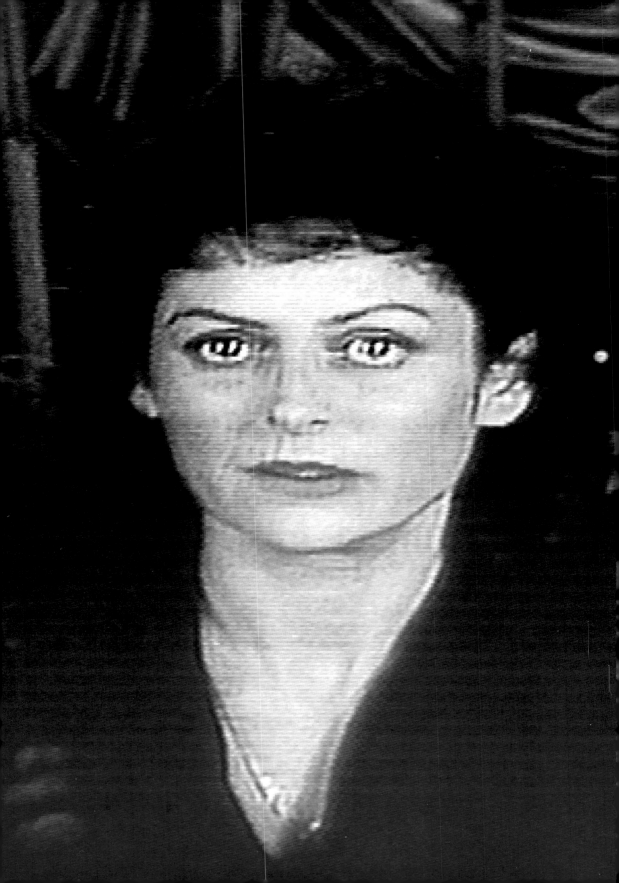

Surface Tension

Essay by Atom Egoyan

Each surface is an interface between two environments that is ruled by a constant activity in the form of an exchange between the two substances placed in contact with one another.

Paul Virilio, 'The Overexposed City'

The idea of surface, when associated with the depiction of character, suggests superficiality and lack of dimension. We tend to think of a surface as something that is without depth, something that offers nothing more than what is immediately visible. On closer reading, however, the concept of surface proves to be the most complex and intriguing aspect of any rendering of personality.

Conceptual issues arising from the notion of surface, especially as it relates to dimensions of personal history and psychological territory, have always challenged the dramatist. But twentieth-century technologies such as film and video have brought an entirely new set of meanings not only to the way in which we communicate with each other, but also to our portrayal of ideas about communication and the effects of communication on our lives.

HOUSEKEEPER
And then, there are those who complain that you're not vocal enough. I'm not talking about noises here, or anything crude.

Noises or anything crude aside, human beings have always found a way to communicate. Alphabets have been introduced, languages have been developed, and stories have been told, printed and read. But the introduction of the cinema screen, like the television screen many years later, presented an entirely new source of information. Even when the images received from these new devices are directly related to personal history — as in the case of home videos — the screen is rarely seen as

Essay

much more than a *conveyor*. While a person reading a letter from a loved one interprets the words on the page as signifiers of emotion — reading *into* the letter associative images that words, by their nature, withhold — a person seeing a projected image of a loved one is, for the most part, seeing just the image: nothing more and nothing less.

> PRODUCER
> It's not difficult to make each other's
> lives more complicated.

We rarely consider the ways in which the intrinsic properties of the projected image may affect our emotional and psychological response to what we perceive. While we recognize that an image can serve as a trigger for a multitude of associations, we are reluctant to admit that these associations may refer back to the image itself. We refuse to recognize that our experience of certain feelings is a direct result of our inability to fully confront what it means to watch a mechanical image. How much of the nostalgia we feel when watching an artifact of personal memorabilia has its source in the sad realization that we have come to need such devices to retain these experiences? How do we distinguish our feelings of loss from these mechanical memories and the experiences they refer to? (One current advertising slogan suggests that photographic evidence helps make 'memories come alive.')

> EDDY
> You see what I mean about it being
> a bit tricky?

> LISA
> I lost my objectivity.

> EDDY
> That can happen.

We treat the idea that a projected image can be a *container*, rather than a *conveyor* of emotion, with uncertainty and confusion. We don't want to consider the implications of the projected image's status as a *container*, since that involves a greater responsibility on our part. A *conveyed* image is brought to us, the viewers. A *contained* image has to be sought out, beyond the glimpse of its surface that a screen affords.

LANCE

What's the matter?

CLARA

That's not what I wrote.

LANCE

What do you mean?

CLARA

They've changed my script.

We believe what most images confirm: what we see is what we get. In keeping with this idea, most representations of human beings on film are modelled on the premise of 'screen presence.' The concept of screen presence assumes that certain actors have the power to allay our deepest suspicions about watching projected images by making us forget the mechanics of the process and lose ourselves in their features. These magically sculpted faces invite our identification. We spontaneously project our personal and collective mythologies onto these faces. They evoke in us an irresistible and compulsive urge to belong.

CLARA

They'll cast you, and ... you'll meet
the producer. He won't listen to me.
He might listen to you.

LANCE

Why?

CLARA

Because you're an actor. You can suggest things you think your character
might do.

LANCE

And if he doesn't listen?

CLARA

You can threaten to leave.

Essay

The face and gestures of the star express a multitude of feelings and fantasies. All the viewer needs to do — in fact, what the viewer can't help but do — is reduce himself to the most primitive responsibility of any watcher: to stare and forget.

> LANCE
> But I'm nothing to them.

> CLARA
> Not until they start shooting. Then
> you're worth a lot.

In such cases, the surface as Virilio defines it is virtually non-existent. The viewer loses himself completely to the screen image; by relinquishing all activity he also gives up the possibility of an exchange. When the screen image *contains* something more immediate to the viewer (a loved one, for example) a true surface can be developed if the viewer breaks the impassive nature of the screen identification process with a degree of involvement. This involvement may be internalized — the image may trigger a memory of an event or a conversation — or it may find more overt manifestations.

> LISA
> *(returning videocassette)*
> I saw things. Things I hadn't seen
> before.

> EDDY
> What? Other meanings?

> LISA
> Yes.

> EDDY
> I guess that's normal.

> LISA
> And other scenes.

EDDY

That's not possible.

❖

In *Speaking Parts*, two women go to the extreme of forming a relationship with a loved one who exists entirely through image. Clara, whose
brother has died donating a lung to his sister, is reduced to watching this
lost figure in video images she has stored in an archival mausoleum.
Lisa is haplessly infatuated with Lance, who steadfastly ignores her ad-
vances. As a result, Lisa is reduced to renting videos of movies that
Lance appears in as an extra, and obsessively waiting for that moment
when her gaze can fix on the object of her desire, searching Lance out
and isolating him from the crowd.

LISA

This is my lover.

EDDY

Ya?

LISA

He's an actor.

Neither of these women is content to merely watch these images
at her leisure, in the comfort of her own home, on her VCR. Even
though Lisa's viewings take place at her apartment, she refuses to make
a 'Best of Lance' compilation tape. The ritualized way she views these
cassettes (paying to rent them out, bringing them home, lighting can-
dles around the television, returning the tapes unwound as soon as she
finds Lance's image) is as baroque in its design as the video mausoleum
Clara visits to see her images of her deceased brother.

LISA

I like to watch his scenes.

EDDY

Uh-huh. So he's your …?

29

LISA

He's my lover.

In order to make these images more meaningful — to invest them with a significance that they, as *conveyors* of information, can only partially realize — the very process of watching these images has to be elaborated. By finding an artificial way of making her images elusive, by rarifying them as a commodity, Lisa reproduces her feeling of romantic pursuit and capture. The images transcend their technological origins and become signifiers of her emotional state. They come, in this way, to *contain* her own feelings and fantasies (while *conveying* these feelings to the viewer).

LISA

I'm in love.

EDDY

What about him?

LISA

You don't believe me.

EDDY

I didn't say that.

A cinematic moment can transcend its limitations as an image and work its way into a viewer's subconscious only if the viewer is able to 'frame' the image in a manner similar to that of these two women. That is, the viewer must consciously acknowledge that he is observing an image, and must make an active, *self*-conscious decision to absorb it. By making this enormous conceptual leap, the viewer identifies with the image and forms a passage of exchange. The screen becomes a surface.

EDDY

But he's just an extra.

LISA

What do you mean?

EDDY
Well, he may be in these movies, but
he doesn't have a speaking part.

LISA *stares at* EDDY.

EDDY
He doesn't talk in them.

LISA
He's on screen.

EDDY *smiles.* LISA *reaches for the photo-résumé and takes it back.*

LISA
There's nothing special about words.

⁂

None of these ideas is in any way intended to minimize the tremendous task set before the screen actor. While theories about technological devices, mediators and the artificiality of the film frame are critical for analysis of the formal qualities of a film, there is no question that in any screen drama the actor is the most direct conduit of a viewer's response.

The actor has a clear choice to make in the interpretation of a given character: whether to attach himself to the most obvious and 'identifiable' qualities of a given role, or to focus on the fringes of what constitutes that personality. By taking this latter route, the actor 'frames' his own performance, allowing, once again, a higher degree of interaction with the viewer. Rather than inviting the viewer to lose himself in a screen presence, the actor asks the viewer to question what it is about the character he's *supposed* to identify with. In this way, a more profound relationship can be established.

PRODUCER
(*watching* LANCE *on monitor*)
You're sure?

CLARA
Yes.

Essay

> PRODUCER
> He's what you're looking for?

> CLARA
> Exactly.

> PRODUCER
> You find him natural enough?

CLARA *nods*.

In *Speaking Parts*, the Producer defends his alterations to Clara's script, claiming that while the story of a man who dies donating his lung to save his sister's life is clearly 'tragic,' Clara's version of the episode is not sufficiently 'dramatic' for the television film he wishes to make.

> PRODUCER
> I just want to make sure that we're
> working with the best script possible.
> Do you understand?

> LANCE
> But it's a personal story …

> PRODUCER
> Of course it is. It's a very personal
> story, and I respect that. I just want
> to make sure that it works *as* a story.
> That's my job.

By structuring his film on the format of a television talk show, the Producer is actually proposing an innovative approach to what is most probably — judging from the moments we have heard during Clara's audition of Lance — a banal script. The idea of the talk show is an attempt to challenge the dramatic format the Producer is working with.

> PRODUCER
> A movie that takes the form of a talk
> show is very original, Lance. I'd
> watch it. And people have always

watched what I'd like to watch. You
have. Ever since you were a kid.
Right?

LANCE *nods.*

By framing Clara's story with the self-conscious device of a talk
show, the Producer hopes to build a surface with his viewer. The
Producer's idea is, in fact, a genuinely exciting and innovative approach
to the material.

> PRODUCER
> What I want you to do is pretend
> that this is a real show. As if it were
> being broadcast live, and you are ac-
> tual participants.

What taints our appreciation of the Producer's motives is our understanding of how Clara suffers under his machinations. The conflict
between our belief that the talk-show telefilm has the makings of a
'good' image and our suspicion that this format will betray the image's
origin in Clara's personal history puts us in a very delicate and provoca-
tive position.

> PRODUCER
> The topic of the show is organ trans-
> plants … Obviously, I need the ten-
> sion level here to be quite high. A
> number of you sitting in the front
> rows have been told that you have
> relatives or children who are in need
> of donors. And the actors sitting up
> here are doctors who specialize in
> the type of operations that could save
> the lives of your loved ones.

How much weight should we give to any character's history, especially once that history has been surrendered to the illusionistic properties of image reproduction? What value does the 'true source' have
when the processed result is more visually dynamic and worthy? Clara

Essay

relates her 'real story' to Lance via the monitor in the video-conference room. Is this presentation any more substantial than the television show the Producer is making? Is one 'talking head' worth more than another? Can any representation of a human being in *Speaking Parts* — whether on video or film — be taken at face value? What does 'face value' mean when all the faces are so carefully composed and lit to be as dramatically amplified as possible within a frame?

> PRODUCER
> It's obvious that David isn't the only person in this country suffering from this disease, but he is certainly the only one lucky enough to be on national television.

The only avenues of emotional connection in the film are created during those moments when one of the women's fantasy images matches the image she is witnessing on the screen. When Lisa finds Lance in the crowd scenes of the rented videos, when Clara gazes at the image of her brother in the mausoleum, or at Lance, an actor she wants to portray her brother, the women's faces express a sense of attachment and love.

> CLARA
> You took a chance.

> LANCE
> Yes.

> CLARA
> Do you do that often?

> LANCE
> What?

> CLARA
> Take chances.

LANCE

Sometimes.

CLARA

When they're interesting.

But these moments are fleeting, if only because they involve projected images that are time-based and must come to an end. The desire expressed by both these women to elaborate these images, to learn how to *make* their own images, will be the source of their personal *unmaking*. Their dream of gaining control over image production is doomed to failure because their relationship to images is not founded on the idea of the image as cultural artifact, but on the ideal of the image as an extension of fantasy and personal mythology.

LISA

I was just about to watch one of your movies. I was wondering if you wanted to drop by.

LANCE *doesn't respond.*

LISA

I know you don't think they're anything special.... But I do.

Tragically (to use the Producer's expression), Clara and Lisa over-invest themselves in the images of their dreams, and lose sight of themselves in the process.

⁜

Film is capable of operating, simultaneously, on at least two different levels. It can present characters, actions and locations in a literal manner that is overwhelmingly realistic and pleasing to watch. But the camera also functions on a more profound level, allowing certain images to situate themselves within the viewer's subconscious. It can be a tool for manipulating ideas about dimension, thus allowing a film not merely to depict, but to transform, to distance and to intensify our perception of reality.

Essay

> CLARA
>
> I hope this isn't too strange for you.

> LANCE
>
> No. *(he laughs)* Did you have a good
> trip?

> CLARA
>
> Fine.

At these moments, the surface of the screen allows degrees of recognition, compassion and transcendence that provoke our expectations and confirm the complexity of watching images in the late twentieth century.

> LANCE
>
> I missed you.

> CLARA
>
> Really?

> LANCE
>
> Yes.

LANCE *and* CLARA *stare at each other on the screens.*

Emotional Logic

Marc Glassman Interviews Atom Egoyan

MARC GLASSMAN: We're talking at length about your career to date and reflecting it through the prism of one film, *Speaking Parts*. The script takes up the major portion of this book, so it seems reasonable to start our conversation by asking you how much of the meaning presented in the film was already apparent for you in the script. In the film Lisa (played by Arsinée Khanjian) says, 'There's nothing special about words.' When you were working on the script, how important were the words? How important were the visuals? Where does the meaningful interplay occur?

ATOM EGOYAN: The whole question of meaning is something that I'm constantly flummoxed by. When one has a vision that requires a very precise framework one is always searching for justifications, for the rationale behind any given decision. Yet one is also aware that that could turn against itself. A very well-developed argument is all it takes to paralyze the whole process. If I'm not careful I can become incapable of writing or directing or conceptualizing. On the one hand my approach has been academic (although I resist that because I don't think of myself as an academic or intellectual filmmaker), but I do realize that in order for me to begin an emotional investigation, I have to create a structure that reflects the thematic of the film within the script itself. There has to be an approach, and it comes down to what the camera represents, what the camera is suggesting by its presence, by its absence or by the nature of its gaze.

For me it's not a simple process of recording dramatic action. There is some interplay with the lens which contributes — not in a purely pictorial sense, but in a more mysterious and elusive way — to what is going on. Those are the moments that really draw me to making images: I feel I can create a texture and a resonance through the act of making the photographic representations iconographic and yet not so iconographic that they're overwhelmed by a formalistic conceit. There is still some life in them. But people are aware of the fact that they are being recorded.

That knowledge that something is being recorded can be very overt, as in *Speaking Parts*. In that film a lot of the behaviour is modulated by the facts that Lance is a performer and that films and home videos are being created throughout the film. In many cases, the people are performing for the camera, which they know is recording them and transmitting their images. I think my characters all possess a degree of self-consciousness, and I find that that is in some way the twentieth-century state of being. We're all self-conscious, we're all aware of the archetypes we draw from in our behavioural patterns. We're all aware of images that we've seen that chronicle or depict behavioural states that we try to replay. The question of whether or not that renders our actions natural or unnatural lies at the core of my desire to make films.

M G: Having looked at *Speaking Parts* a lot recently, it seems to me that the apparent confrontation between video and film is a red herring. I don't see video as the pivotal element. Did you intend the video sequences to mean something significantly different from everything else in the film?

A E: I use video as a launching pad when characters veer off from being wholly rational. It can suggest a dream state, memory, hallucinations. It's really a springboard. There are times when it is used in a purely literal way, and there are times when the camera moves in onto the pixels, and one becomes very aware of the construct of the image. Then one has to see it as a phantasmagoric phenomenon.

Sometimes when one watches these scenes one can think of the video in terms of a surrealistic device, but I hope it goes beyond that. In *Family Viewing*, the very texture at times was suspect. The scenes in the condominium were shot on video, but there was no literal mechanical device that could have created those particular images. So they took on a metaphorical significance, they became a reflection of a state of mind. In *Speaking Parts*, video is treated in a more literal way. I think that the moments where it slips into fantasy are much clearer. There isn't as much ambiguity.

I confess that some of the change in *Speaking Parts* grew out of my dismay at seeing *Family Viewing* on video. I realized that when one tries to work with textures, one has to keep in mind that although these films may work with audiences when they're projected, a large number of people will only see the work on video. The problem with video in *Family Viewing* is that the device is too subtle. The film doesn't work on home video on the terms on which it was designed to work. It's easier to watch on home video because one isn't aware of the tension of watching these degraded images and watching the very monolithic cutting style in the condominium scenes. One's not aware that it's strange. It just seems comfortable. But if one watches it in a film theatre it certainly strikes one as being disturbing. In *Speaking Parts*, I wanted the devices I was using to be able to explain themselves even on the television screen. It's possible to watch *Speaking Parts* on home video and get a full sense of what the film is trying to explore. If that means I have to be a bit less subtle about how I'm working with textures, then that's just one of the disadvantages of video.

I'm pleased that *Speaking Parts* is now on laser disc because it's possible to retrieve some of the detailing. A filmmaker is always at the mercy of bad dubs. I do really like those moments in *Family Viewing* where the boy reaches up to change the dial on his monitor in the nursing home. If you're watching on the TV set then he's reaching up for your dial as well. It's a shocking moment. I used to write films as projected images on a screen, not as home video. I'm more aware of video now. It wasn't a market I had in mind when I was making *Family Viewing*. Both *Family Viewing* and *Speaking Parts* have found a much larger market on video and laser disc than they did in theatres.

There are two copies of *Speaking Parts* in every Blockbuster Video store in the States, which gives it the kind of distribution that didn't occur here or in U.S. cinemas. I was speaking in Montreal and someone from a small town in Nova Scotia said that the copy of *Family Viewing* in his local video store was the subject of a lot of discussion. That anecdote suggests to me that there is a viable way of distributing that type of film. I guess a filmmaker starting a career now would take that as a given, but I have been working during the time when that transition was being made.

MG: *Speaking Parts'* plot involves an affair between a scriptwriter, Clara (played by Gabrielle Rose), and an actor, Lance (played by Michael McManus). You have Lance audition a bit of the script for Clara, and you even have the Producer (played by David Hemblen) act as a re-write man on the script. Let's talk about that alternative script, and the Producer's 're-write.' How far did you carry the notion of that script?

AE: That script is something that I actually wrote for Gabrielle to look at. It's really a banal melodrama. One of the curious aspects of our media-saturated society is that we begin to think that a media image has a currency outside of its fairly practical purposes. We think that when things are elevated to the level of transmitted image they gain in importance and significance in relation to our own experience. I loved the idea of Clara's character: someone who had had this phenomenal event in her life and who was plagued by guilt. What could she do to create a tribute to her brother, this missing person? The fact that she ritualistically goes to watch his image in a 'video mausoleum' easily segued into the idea that she could take what that image meant and turn it into a commercially viable image, a film.

MG: The environment that you create in *Speaking Parts* is one in which alienation is highly evident. What sort of society were you trying to delineate, or critique, in the film?

AE: *Speaking Parts* tries to chronicle different stratas of people who are infatuated with each other and whose lives are structured through media. There is Eddy, the king of domestic video: he makes home videos and distributes mainstream ones at a store. Then there's the David Hemblen character, a TV and film producer who is obviously operating at a much wider level of distribution. That creates a class structure: the Producer can use the fact that he's made it and take that as a given. Remember when he tells Lance, and I'll paraphrase: 'Images that I've made have become part of your subconscious, therefore you must respect me'? That's a fundamental way of outlining a class superiority. His authority as a Producer goes beyond the level of questioning. 'I'm here because of certain things that I've done, and you must submit to my authority because those things have become an inexorable part of your experience.' It doesn't matter what shows he produced (and Lance becomes too intimidated to ask what they were). In the film industry, that happens all the time. People want to know what you've done. Very often, I don't have to say what I've done, I just have to say who's distributed it, or where it's been seen. What a show is about or what a filmmaker has actually accomplished artistically are secondary to what sort of airplay or distribution a film has had and how many people have seen it. I love that backdrop to the film: all the people are fighting for their own identities, but the currency with which they're fighting is the projected images they're receiving or trying to make. And make on their own terms, sometimes succeeding and sometimes failing. I still continue to present characters who are engaged in the act of making images of each other. *Calendar* is about that. It's endlessly fascinating for me. In *Calendar*, the images include photographs for a calendar, home video and film. If I couldn't continue to explore these ideas, I probably wouldn't be making films.

In the society I've depicted in *Speaking Parts,* there are producers and there are watchers. There are many reasons why that society is segregated into those two camps, but there are very particular rules in *Speaking Parts*. Why watchers want to be producers is easy to understand, but why they are prevented from doing so becomes a very interesting political issue. It has to do with the fact that certain types of images are more accessible than others. Why is it that certain people are able to channel their feelings through the media and have those ideas and emotions communicated at a mass level while other people are marginalized? Does it have to do with the psychological fabric of those characters? How much of it has to do with the technology they can get their hands on?

In terms of my own situation, I've seen my work grow from very marginal audiences to more mainstream audiences. What is the rationale for that? Is it because I've been able to afford more expensive cameras, better sound systems? Is it because my vision has matured? These are very interesting questions. *Speaking Parts* was a way of exploring them in a contained drama.

MG: The TV talk show, with the Producer acting as the host, is staged near the end of the film. It's an intricate and resonant scene. How did you devise it?

AE: As I was plotting the film, I realized I loved the idea of the TV show, where I could take an issue that is fictional but create a format that people are used to identifying with. On 'real' TV talk shows, there's a level of interaction between the audience and the guests. In *Speaking Parts* I'm preventing the audience from reaching that 'normal' level of interaction because I've assigned conflicting roles to all of the characters they are seeing. The resulting confusion on the part of the viewer is something that thrills me. The viewer doesn't quite know what it is he's watching.

The most resonant moments for me as a viewer always come when I don't quite know what it is I'm watching. I'm lost in a wash of emotions and feelings that don't originate from something that I can identify immediately. They're the most exhilarating passages in cinema because they come so close to the dream state. Cinema has the ability to transport us into other worlds, but for a number of reasons I'll never understand, we are taught to regard those moments in a film with a lot of suspicion. If something is to be a dream state, it has to be signalled in a very specific way: most obviously, there's a shot of a character rustling around in his bed at night, cut to an image, then cut to him rustling around a bit more, cut to the image. It's so clichéd it's absurd, but it's still used as a device. It's as though we can't allow ourselves to disengage our rational selves and just drift with the film.

MG: Did the script for *Speaking Parts* immediately follow *Family Viewing*?

AE: Scripts are developed and rejected between films. I find that the most informative part of the process is writing an entire script that I reject because I've decided that something's just not interesting enough to pursue. It's not worth my passion, or there aren't enough reasons to make it into a film. It exists too neatly as a script; it doesn't necessarily open up possibilities or avenues for exploration as cinema. I'm at that stage right now. I've written a script that I've decided to reject. It's an important part of the filmmaking process.

MG: When you finally started on the script for *Speaking Parts*, how long did it take for it to cohere into something that you wanted to make into a film?

AE: It developed over about six months. I've always had in mind a film set in a hotel because I worked in a hotel for a long time. The original draft dealt with a relationship between two people who work in the hotel housekeeping department. That was the springboard. It was Lance and Lisa originally. It developed from there. I loved the idea of a person being infatuated with someone who fails to recognize that person's existence. The idea of Lance being an extra was always there as well. In the first drafts I made a lot more of Lisa visiting Lance on shoots and always being pushed away. There were scenes of her trying to coax marginal people on the film crew to give him a speaking part. There were a lot more anonymous casting sessions — where Lance wouldn't know what he was applying for but he would be reading various lines into a camera — auditions that never came to fruition. That was the whole film. It didn't have enough resonance. It didn't have the dramatic drive for a feature film. Clara appeared in the second draft, as did the Producer.

MG: How about Clara? Was she a totally original creation or does she have some basis in people you've encountered in the film industry?

AE: Clara is based on a woman who had a screenplay (I get sent a lot of screenplays). In this woman's case, I had to confront someone who had written material that wasn't good but that was obviously based on something that was very close to her. I really tried to find a way of dealing with this person, to communicate that although I was interested in the material I didn't feel the script was well written.

It's difficult to say how things evolve short of giving actual anecdotes about where they come from. *The Adjuster* is very easy to talk about because it was written in the aftermath of an experience that my family had gone through, and it just came in a very lucid flash. The other films deal with figures that are amalgamations of people I know, or are fantasies on experiences I've had. They're riffs. *The Adjuster* is very concrete because the time between the event and the writing of the script was very condensed, a matter of months.

MG: Still, *The Adjuster* has 'riffs' too: the Censor Board, the Adjuster's house, the bizarre couple who invade that home. I find the layering of the stories in *Speaking Parts* to be quite complex. How did the final script evolve?

AE: The evolution came about through my interest in developing themes. Here is a question: can people live through imagistic representations of life? If they can, do they then need to gain control of how those representations are made? And if these questions can be answered 'yes' and 'yes,' at what point do people fall in love with the representation of the loved one? Maybe they are really falling in love with their own ability to conjure up that image. Does the love then become narcissistic? I find little satisfaction in having characters proposing these ideas literally, so I try to find a structure that brings up these issues.

MG: *Speaking Parts* is a complicated narrative with a number of intertwining plots. Did you have any organizing principles when it came time to structure the script?

AE: It was a question of seeing material and trying to go back to a notion of counterpoint. I'd develop the theme and certain voices that articulate that theme by playing with it and creating tensions between two disparate tracks, which are ultimately reflecting or mirroring a common concern. That's the notion of counterpoint in musical as well as narrative structures.

A fugal structure is a greater articulation of that: in baroque music there's the ground bass, a repeating bass line, which often becomes the foundation of the piece. That's what distinguishes the music of Purcell from that of Bach. Purcell had a heavy reliance on the ground bass, on the repeating theme at the bottom, while Bach — a composer I adore — was able to create as much surprise and variety in the ground bass as in the other voices. I don't know how far I can extend the analogy, but in *Speaking Parts* the repeating theme is people's relationship to each other in a world obsessed by representation. Each element can be seen to heighten the other strand. I find I'm drawn to the fugual form. It comes very naturally to me because of my musical training.

I don't know how much of the structuring is conscious when I'm writing. I think that I work my way through material, and for me it's just a question of what sustains my interest. At what point do I feel the need to switch channels to something else? In fact, one could see my films as fugual, but one could also see them as being structured around channel-hopping. A scene appears for a while, and then one switches to something else. It's almost as though one's switching between two different programs, and at some point they're married. I've been influenced by counterpoint in music, but I've probably been just as influenced by channel-hopping as a kid. I don't know which has had the greater impact on my work.

MG: It seems to me that each film is a process of exploration for you. Do you find that certain characters and situations on the page almost incite you to start filming?

AE: Yes, they're teasing me, and I know that I cannot be satisfied with what they're proposing on a page. I know that the act of filming people playing these parts is going to bring to the thematic a dimension that exceeds my imagination, and that's an important thing. One can read a script and imagine what it's going to be like, but that isn't enough for me. It isn't enough to imagine how these characters could come alive, as the saying goes. I want to become more alive by watching them being filmed, and I want to experience the tension that is going to be part of what I'm going to say. I'm never drawn to characters who just seem to yell out 'represent me.' I'm attracted to people who are lost in a world that I can navigate. I have to be able to show the characters' attempts at gaining aspects of personality and engage the viewer in a concomitant process of discovery.

MG: You've got the script. Who do you cast? Do you write for particular people? Are you looking for another adventure by exploring these mysterious characters with new performers?

AE: Choosing actors is an absolutely essential part of the process. Some are new to me and some I return to. Actors are phenomenal, because they are there to defend their characters. In *Speaking Parts* that becomes an interesting conceit in itself. I found that the actors would defend what they saw as the emotional logic behind behaviour patterns or activities. I can write stuff, and I can have people go through weird contortions to get to certain points, but the actor is the person who will actually test the character and make sure that it makes emotional sense and isn't just a dramatic contrivance. That's very important for me: that an actor can see his way through a character who (in my films especially) goes through some very extreme states of behaviour. Take the scene with Gabrielle Rose, the one where she breaks down. The way she does that is thrilling to me. I'm just amazed by it. Arsinée's scene with the bride. The way that came across thrills me.

MG: Did you intend Arsinée to play Lisa?

AE: No, that's the funny thing. Arsinée gets full credit for getting the role because originally I wanted her to play Clara, but she wanted to be Lisa. She was so insistent that we eventually auditioned her for that part, and that's how she got it. It was supposed to be the other way around. Gabrielle was supposed to play Lisa. That seems remarkable now.

MG: I find Lisa to be a real stretch for Arsinée: that character is so unlike her as a person.

AE: That's the surprising thing about all of Arsinée's performances. People are always surprised to meet her because she's so open and so spontaneous with her ideas and feelings. In the films, up to now, she's always been trapped in some character. She's not in my new one, *Calendar*. In that film she plays someone much freer with herself, much more easily identifiable. That sense of freedom permeates the entire film. *Calendar* is probably the most enjoyable film I've made.

MG: Do you have a set manner in which you work with actors?

AE: Not at all. There are some actors who want to have a very meticulous, analytical breakdown of why their character is behaving in a certain way, and then there are others who don't want to talk very much and don't want to rehearse. I have to be receptive to both types of performers. I like to rehearse a lot. When we're dealing with a lot of text and ideas it's often very important to develop a whole interior script to which an actor can refer. But there are some performers who I've worked with who will just intuit their way through and don't have to have anything explained to them. I have to make myself shut up — which is not easy for me to do — but sometimes that's what the actors need. Anyone from a theatrical background is used to discussing things, and most of the actors I've worked with have had that background. Elias Koteas, who played the Adjuster, actually prefers to work on the intuitive level. He doesn't want to rehearse too much. He really wants to feel a scene as it happens at that moment. I have to create a space for that. There are people who find the way I articulate my ideas to be completely bewildering. There is an approach to all my films that is very simple and emotional, and they do follow an emotional logic. It's possible to see the films on those terms and not get caught up in a lot of the other issues that I like to talk about.

It's difficult for me to talk about emotional representations on film because I find them to be so self-evident. *Speaking Parts* is almost operatic, isn't it? The way emotions are conveyed, emotional states of mind, notions of need and desire and longing and rejection: these conceits are the basis for making the film. But I don't want to talk about those things because they're beyond discussion. I take those as givens.

MG: I'm intrigued by the character of the Adjuster. How much of that personality was worked out in advance? How much was a response to the intuitive nature of your actor, Elias Koteas?

AE: That character follows a certain pattern which I seem to have established for male leads. They are always people who drift through space without ever knowing their potential to affect other people. What I found strong about the Adjuster was the way his job could automatically transport him to the level of myth. He could suddenly become an angel of reconstruction, of rematerialization, by descending on people's lives and redirecting their energies while they are absolutely devastated. They could completely lose themselves to him for two weeks or so to get their claim and then either stay his friend or drop him. That character was very clear in my mind. It's a character I could understand. It had nothing to do with an adjuster.

Elias was really important, because if that character were played by someone who seemed completely cognizant of his effect on other people, someone who displays his analytical ability through his eyes — John Malkovich or William Hurt, for example — it would not have had the same effect. It would have seemed as if this character knew what he was doing, was somehow driven by it for very clear and perhaps malicious reasons. What I liked about Elias from the other films he'd done was his very open quality. He's emotional but not fixed in any particular type of mindset that could categorize him as being manipulative. That's what the whole film toys with: is he manipulating these people or are they manipulating him? It was very important to have an actor whose presence could keep that ambiguity open. With a lot of actors it would have fallen on the side of him manipulating these people.

MG: The difference between Elias in *The Adjuster* and your other leads is that he is far more intense. An audience does care for the Adjuster in a more connected way than it does for Michael McManus's Lance in *Speaking Parts*. Was that your intent?

AE: It has a lot to do with my relationship with the actor. Elias is a very emotional person. The kind of direction I gave him had to be rooted in that. There are aspects of Elias's personality that I think endow that character with a level of emotionality that really excited me. That's why I wanted to use him. Michael has a different personality that was perfectly in keeping for what I wanted in *Speaking Parts*.

I think actors are receptive to any project. The question is whether one has access to them, whether one can bypass the various screens that they have set up to protect themselves from the public at large. Actors are always really excited about taking risks. I don't think the financial consideration is as important as others think it is. What's more important is letting the actors know that I'm around and that my interest in their participation is not limited to their marquee value but has something to do with what they possess as personalities.

MG: You came to film out of theatre and music. Why not be a theatre director?

AE: Once I got onto the idea of the camera, and the idea of the camera being a possible participant and character, I felt that in some ways it allowed me to become more private. Film by nature doesn't require the same type of interaction as the theatre. It's a much more solitary experience, watching a film, than going to a theatrical presentation. It suited my vision. I also felt that in a lot of the drama I was writing I was just treading over material that other people had done. I was so influenced by Pinter or Beckett that I never really found my own voice in the drama I was doing. It was easier for me to feel confident about my direction and scripting when I was making films. I was able to absorb influences, let them pass through me and grow outside of them more easily than I could with theatre.

MG: Some critics have referred to your scripts as hermetic. Do you think that a general audience can comprehend the motivation behind some of your narrative strategies?

AE: That's a very big question for me. I have to believe that they can. The films become much richer when one is able to position philosophical arguments into the narrative. I realize that people are not necessarily trained to recognize those questions, so my films can also be appreciated on other terms, simple emotional terms. How many people watching David Cronenberg's work are familiar with Cartesian philosophy? Very few. But if a viewer does know Descartes, that adds another level of appreciation to the work. My lack of familiarity with Cartesian philosophy made it impossible to know how seriously I should take Cronenberg's earlier films. At a certain point I just trust myself to the vision of someone whose work I like and respect.

MG: There's something ineffable about the relationship between an artist and an audience. How do you see it?

AE: It's about taking myself and a group of people on a journey to a place that they have not seen or felt before but which rings with a truth or authenticity for reasons that surprise me. There's an unknown energy that either works or it doesn't. And then, when the doors within these rooms open for people to drift in and lose themselves, there is extraordinary potential for interaction. It's an interactive process because there is so much dreaming and projecting onto my images; people want them to operate in so many different ways. They want things to be better paced, or they want some actor to look better, or they want someone to do something that's going to throw them. They cannot change the course of these images; it's inexorable. They have to commit themselves to the way these things unfold. That tension between what the viewer would like to think is happening and what is actually happening can create convergences that are impossible to consider in other art forms.

I don't think the filmmaker is always in control of that tension or interaction with the audience. The films that really excite me are those in which it is unclear if the filmmaker is really aware of how disturbing or moving the image is. The filmmaker just felt the image at that moment, but its implications are overwhelmingly beautiful or monstrous or hideous. The image provokes these reactions because it is calling on something primal.

MG: In experimental films and videos, questions of texture or sound are often preeminent. In your films, although narrative concerns have precedence, similar questions arise out of your aesthetic interests. In fact, some of these issues of texture occur within the script itself. You're making pictures that carry coded messages that move the notion of the narrative forward. Will audiences appreciate and decode your stories?

AE: Well, I hope so. That's why I'm making films. I approach my own subject matter and the way I direct my own scripts completely differently from the way in which I direct other people's scripts. When I apply my directorial talents to someone else's material, the question becomes: how do I best serve the material? How can I convey the ideas in a cinematic way? When I did *Gross Misconduct*, the CBC biography of hockey player Brian Spencer, there were aspects of his life that drew me to the project. For instance, Spencer's father was ritualistically shot to death by the RCMP at a TV studio while he was trying to see his son's first game in a national broadcast. The subject matter appealed to me, but it would have been problematic to take my approach and apply it to the script since that aspect of Spencer's history was just part of its structure, not its preponderant reason for being a script. If I were to write that script it would be completely different. When I've directed for other people I have paid close attention to style; the camera has been an active participant but in a more classical way than it is in my own films. My films are, to a certain extent, a reaction against the type of filmmaking I do in a more mercenary way. I make my images and code languages in a very specific way. When I'm making my own films I have the highest possible expectations of my audience. I have to think they look at films the same way I look at films.

MG: In the case of *Gross Misconduct*, did they allow you a fairly free hand to re-write?

AE: To re-structure. The film as it exists is structured quite differently from the original script. I worked on that with Paul Gross, the writer. I proposed my idea of the structure and he incorporated it into the final scenario.

MG: *Speaking Parts* features one of your favourite character actors in a showy role. David Hemblen is superb as the Producer, a slightly sinister figure who always seems to be in complete control of events. How much of your own experiences as a director were worked into that part?

AE: A lot of the things he says I can't help but hear myself saying in my professional life. He says (paraphrasing my own script), 'Clara's script was something that was very important to her, something that she went through, but that wasn't what interested me, it wasn't what I felt other people wanted to hear.' He embodies that approach of taking certain elements of people's lives but getting rid of their point of view. I find it very funny when he says, 'This script is so important that not only am I going to produce it, I am also going to act in it.' He's really going all the way. That scene in the TV studio where he has to communicate to the actors who they are, what they're about, that sort of little dance to get them excited, that's what every director does. It's part of the whole absurdity of filmmaking. I could be in the most rotten mood ever and I still have to get a shooting day made. When I am on the set, I find myself twisting in the most extraordinary contortions to get people excited and revved up. The whole issue of manipulating reality and exaggerating and twisting and bending and making things fit one's notion of dramaturgy at the risk of any real authenticity is part of the process. I'm constantly doing it.

Another factor that influenced the creation of the Producer was a very strange experience I had when I was directing the pilot for 'Friday the 13th.' I had a lot of conversations with the producer of that series. He was in L.A., and we would have sessions at the end of the day. He would have the rushes on VHS, and I would phone and listen to him watching the rushes. I'd be on conference call. There would be a number of executives from the studio watching the rushes I'd made, and they'd all be commenting freely, as they were watching, to me at the other end. I'd be giving explanations or I'd be taking notes and after a while I thought, this is very odd. This producer was like the Producer in *Speaking Parts*: he had many projects going at the same time and he was very hands-on. He was intimidating as well. I found that character fascinating.

MG: You've already mentioned the fugue as being an important structural element in the film. I've always found *Speaking Parts* to be more visually elaborate than your previous features. Did you intend the visuals, the sets, the music — the production values — to indicate a progression, economically, from your earlier films?

AE: It's important to realize that as *Speaking Parts* evolved I was dealing with a lot of personal frustration with the people who didn't understand that the devices and textures in *Family Viewing* were the result of a very carefully thought-out plan as opposed to budgetary limitation. That drove me crazy. I'll never forget a journalist who, during the Toronto Festival of Festivals, commented that the acting seemed stilted, the sets looked like sets and the whole work looked like it was shot on bad film stock. Those were three things I had actually paid a lot of attention to, to create! Months later, when the film was building momentum, the same person was doing a profile piece on my work and he asked me, 'How do people usually react to *Family Viewing* when they first see it?' I said, just to test his mettle, 'Some people say, "The acting seemed stilted, the sets looked like sets and it looked like it was shot on bad film stock."' Instead of saying that was the way he felt the first time he saw it, he said, 'Oh really, how could people think that?'

That sort of confusion began to eat at me. I had to create a look for *Speaking Parts* that made it clear that any deviation from the way films normally appear was intentional, and people could not pass it off as 'the budget.' If I had had three times as much money to make *Family Viewing* I would have made it exactly the same way. With *Speaking Parts*, since it deals so much with people being seduced by images, seduced into the world of the image, it was very important that the film images themselves be seductive. I was drawn to the colonial-style hotel and its old-world panelling because they suggested the sophistication of an earlier time. By placing the main action there, I created a counter-effect to the video technology so a viewer was not able to apply the usual reaction to seeing high tech in film, which is that it's somehow futuristic. In order to get that dichotomy across it was important that the environments seemed lush. We worked on that a lot with the production designer to create an effect that would make a viewer want to be in that elegant conference room. We didn't want the locations to seem sterile or cold, even though what goes on in them — video-sex, for example — might have those associations.

MG: What were the budgets for *Family Viewing*, *Speaking Parts* and *The Adjuster*?

AE: My budgets have grown slightly bigger each time. *Family Viewing* was made for $200,000, *Speaking Parts* for $800,000 and *The Adjuster* for $1.5 million. Don't forget I'm fortunate to be working with exceptionally talented people. I rely on the artists I work with to pull off amazing feats for meagre amounts of money.

MG: Some of the people who worked on your earlier films have gone on to direct their own features. Most notably, Peter Mettler directed *The Top of His Head* and *Tectonic Plates*, and Bruce McDonald made *Roadkill* and *Highway 61*. You used Peter Mettler as cinematographer for *Next of Kin* and *Family Viewing* and then worked with Paul Sarossy on *Speaking Parts* and *The Adjuster*. Is it different working with Paul?

AE: I worked with Peter early on in my career. Discussions with him about the camera and its possibilities were crucial to my development. Peter's whole sense of being able to use the camera to record completely intuitive moments is a thrilling concept. It makes cinematography a pure art form.

Every working relationship takes a while to get used to, because you can't help projecting the way you formed a previous relationship on to the new one. Paul is someone who doesn't want to discuss things as much as Peter did. He is definitely in synch with what the material demands, but in a very different way than Peter was. One has to understand that some people don't necessarily find much value in the process of discussing things beforehand, or they find that draining, and that's completely valid. It just takes a greater leap of faith for someone like me who tends to over-articulate things.

Film is weird that way. Before a production starts, there are all these meetings. I meet the key people — the costume designer, the properties designer — and I launch into my harangue about my vision of the film. Then what do I do? Do I wait for them to give me something, or try to check out if I have something in common with them at a personal level? It's a very strange process.

MG: You talked earlier about the operatic quality of *Speaking Parts*. Certainly a major element of that 'operatic' quality is Clara's story, the film within the film. You've commented that you find her own script to be quite banal. How do you think Clara relates to her story?

AE: What's interesting is that she herself does very little to defend her material on an emotional level. When she's asking Lance to defend her idea to the Producer, she says, 'It happened to me and my brother.' That's as close as she gets. She does not talk about what she went through. When the Producer explains to Lance that the script is based on the tragic story of Clara and her brother, Lance realizes for the first time that her brother actually died. Clara doesn't capitalize on this when she's trying to convince Lance. She doesn't try to give him a history or a story that conveys the depths of her emotional despair; she trusts that he will sense it. That is a very curious thing for someone to do with Lance, because he's not entirely capable of feeling someone else's emotions. And it raises a curious issue: to what extent can one trust that someone else will, as Lisa says, 'feel someone else feeling you' when those feelings are mediated, when they have filters and screens? That's what truly interests me in the film, not the mixing of video and film technologies. To what extent can one trust one's identity to someone else feeling what that identity is about?

MG: That's at the core of the film. And the answer in *Speaking Parts*: nobody does.

AE: It's very bleak. No one does, no one can. The most piercing moments — those with the husband and the new bride, or the father breaking down and crying — are held under such scrutiny because everyone else is trying to glean some truth from them. It's funny and yet completely vampiristic.

MG: You briefly commented earlier on one of my favourite scenes in the film. It occurs when Lance has to let Clara know that the character of the sister has been written out of the script. Gabrielle Rose seizes that moment to create an emotionally pure — and chilling — hysterical laugh that gives the audience a look into the depths of her despair.

AE: Do you notice what's actually happening there at the level of texture? Throughout the film, in all the scenes you've seen Clara, you've seen her on monitors looking straight at the camera. In that scene, the coverage is almost mathematical. It's shot and cut so that Lance and Clara appear to be across the table from each other, appear to be looking at each other rather than at monitors. That is the moment at which her breakdown occurs. For me that is such a great thing. Up until that moment you've been seeing this coverage in which a monitor has been so intrinsically involved. Clara and Lance seem to be looking right at each other across a table, but they are actually thousands of miles apart and are looking at screens. Then, at that point, one suspends one's disbelief; one is watching them watching each other as if there were no barriers at all. I don't think a viewer thinks about that when he's watching it, but it was necessary for me to have that idea in mind when I was directing it.

I think that's a good example of the difference between my approach as a director and yours as a critic. For you that scene is 'emotionally pure'; you might not even be aware of all the textural and formally technical things taking place there which for me are profound and very exciting. Yet it was the technical aspect of that scene that allowed me to arrive at that moment of emotional honesty! I could not have come to that moment if I had just thought of it as a pictorial representation of someone breaking down. I need something more to arrive at that emotional moment, to explore something that simple. I have great suspicions about conveying screen emotion. It's my feeling that it can be too easy to just fix the camera on someone going through emotional turmoil. There's something very disturbing about that for me, about my reasons for doing it. I strive to find a structure that allows me to address my own suspicion and still communicate an emotional story. My hope and my dream is that the viewer is involved in all the levels of contradiction and all the levels of complexity that a moment like that actually sustains.

Speaking Parts

An Ego Film Arts Production in association with Don Ranvaud, Telefilm Canada, the Ontario Film Development Corporation, Academy Pictures (Rome) and Film Four International (London).

Writer and Director Atom Egoyan
Director of Photography Paul Sarossy
Art Director Linda Del Rosario
Editor Bruce McDonald
Script Editor Allen Bell
Music Mychael Danna

Starring
Lance Michael McManus
Lisa Arsinée Khanjian
Clara Gabrielle Rose
Eddy Tony Nardi
Producer David Hemblen
Housekeeper Patricia Collins
Father Gerard Parkes
Trish Jacqueline Samuda
Ronnie Peter Krantz

Speaking Parts

1. Exterior. Cemetery. Day.

CLARA, *an attractive woman in her early thirties, approaches a large mausoleum.*

2. Interior. Apartment building. Lisa's apartment. Evening.

LISA, *a woman in her mid-twenties, is watching television in her apartment. She is playing a tape on her VCR. On the television, the tape plays a scene from a movie in which a concert pianist is giving a recital to a crowded hall. The camera moves slowly past* LISA *and onto this scene. In the recital hall, one of the extras playing a member of the audience seems to catch the camera's attention. It is* LANCE, *a strikingly attractive man in his mid-twenties.* LANCE's *features are almost androgynous.*

3. Interior. Mausoleum. Day.

CLARA *approaches the spot where the ashes of her brother,* CLARENCE, *are kept. She stares at the spot on the wall, which is covered with other names. Beside each of these names is a small button.*

4. Interior. Apartment building. Laundry room. Afternoon.

LANCE *enters the tiny room with a basket full of laundry.* LISA *is waiting for him.* LANCE *begins to load his laundry into the washer, ignoring* LISA *completely.* LISA *leaves the room.* LANCE *continues to load his laundry into the machine.*

5. Interior. Mausoleum. Day.

CLARA, *after staring at the spot where* CLARENCE's *ashes are kept, pushes the button beneath the inscription of his name. She moves to a small viewing area inside the mausoleum. A delicate bench stands in front of a television monitor.* CLARA *seats herself on this bench and waits for an image to appear on the monitor.*

Screenplay

6. Interior. Apartment building. Laundry room. Afternoon.

LANCE *moves to the dryer, which he opens. From inside the dryer, he extracts a large bouquet of roses.*

7. Interior. Mausoleum. Day.

CLARA *watches a brief video sequence of her brother* CLARENCE.

8. Interior. Apartment building. Lance's apartment. Evening.

LANCE *at the far end of his apartment. He is arranging the roses in a vase.*

9. Interior. Apartment building. Lisa's apartment. Evening.

LISA *looks at something we don't see.*

10. Interior. Mausoleum. Day.

CLARA *stares at the blank video monitor.*

11. Interior. Hotel. Laundry room. Day.

Close-ups of various items of laundry being sorted. At the end of this sequence, the camera reveals LISA *sorting the dirty linen in the laundry room of a large hotel. Sheets, towels, pillowcases and other items are being sorted by hand as they are expelled from a monstrous chute.*

12. Interior. Hotel. Guest room. Day.

LANCE *is making a bed in a room upstairs. During the day, he is a maid at the hotel. His long hair is untied, and he looks almost exactly like an attractive woman. It is important to stress that* LANCE *is not a transvestite. There is absolutely nothing burlesque or 'campy' about his appearance. It is the casualness with which this transition occurs that is most remarkable, and disturbing. In all scenes outside of the hotel,* LANCE*'s long hair is tied back.*

13. Interior. Hotel. Laundry room. Day.

LISA *pushes a laundry cart out of the laundry room and down a hallway.*

14. Interior. Hotel. Guest room. Day.

LANCE *is scrubbing away at a dirty bidet.*

15. Interior. Hotel. Hallway. Day.

LISA *pushing her laundry cart along one of the hotel hallways.*

LANCE at the headboard of a bed, tucking in the sheets and arranging the pillows. LISA appears behind him. LANCE is startled by LISA's presence.

LISA

Hi.

Pause. LANCE continues to make the bed, ignoring LISA.

LISA

I didn't mean to scare you.

Pause. LISA moves up beside LANCE and presents him with a bundle of hand towels.

LISA

I brought you some hand towels.

LANCE stares at the hand towels.

LISA

They were the last ones. I saved them for you.

LANCE takes the hand towels from LISA. He moves out of the frame. LISA pauses. Her expression is disturbed and lost.

[handwritten annotations:]

Lance should play that these are very important objects, they realize that they are only handtowels.

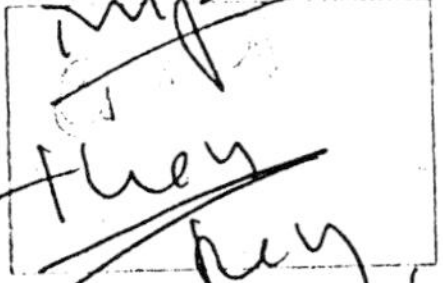

He grabs them here and walks away

unmoved.

he never looks

Boy for us

She talks to herself

Lance is dusting the top of a cabinet. He leaves the duster on the top. LISA steals it.

slow dolly toward the two

Sound of brush overlaps over into 15)

emphasize hand & foot. No faces.

dolly around to

FOOT

shoeshine

CUT TO:

CLARA enters the lobby of the hotel. She moves to the registration desk.

shoeshine.

CUT TO:

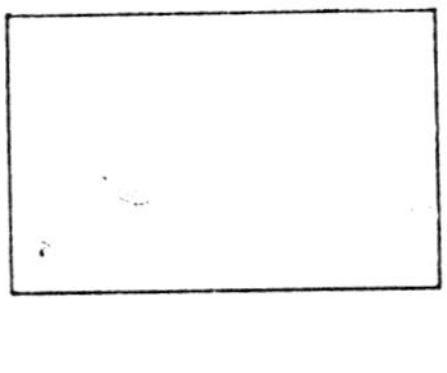

a beautiful invisily shot.

16. Interior. Hotel. Guest room. Day.

LANCE *at the foot of a bed, smoothing the sheets.* LISA *appears behind him.*

> LISA
>
> Hi.

Pause. LANCE *continues to make the bed, ignoring* LISA.

> LISA
>
> I didn't mean to scare you.

Pause. LISA *moves up beside* LANCE *and presents him with a bundle of hand towels.*

> LISA
>
> I brought you some hand towels.

LANCE *stares at the hand towels, and takes them from* LISA.

> LISA
>
> They were the last ones. I saved them
> for you.

LANCE *moves out of the frame.* LISA *pauses. Her expression is disturbed and lost. In the hallway* LANCE *pauses and waits as* LISA *moves out of the room.*

17. Interior. Hotel. Lobby. Early evening.

CLARA *enters the lobby of the hotel. She moves to the registration desk.*

18. Exterior. Cloud Nine video store. Early evening.

LISA *approaches the front entrance of the video store.*

19. Interior. Trendy used-clothing store. Early evening.

LANCE *exploring the various costumes on display in this popular boutique.*

20. Interior. Hotel. Clara's room. Early evening.

CLARA *collapses onto her bed in total exhaustion.*

21. Interior. Cloud Nine video store. Early evening.

LISA *wandering through the rows of videotapes, looking for a particular title.*

Screenplay

In her hand, LISA clutches an eight-by-ten publicity photograph of LANCE. The camera wanders away from LISA and finds EDDY, a clerk at the store. EDDY, who is in his late twenties, is staring at LISA.

22. Interior. Trendy cafeteria. Early evening.

LANCE has positioned himself in a conspicuous place in this crowded establishment. It is clearly the type of place where one goes to be seen, and LANCE enjoys the type of attention he can expect to receive here. LANCE has a full carafe of wine in front of him.

23. Interior. Hotel. Clara's room. Early evening.

CLARA has begun to unpack her luggage. She sets a framed photograph of CLARENCE on the desk.

24. Interior. Apartment building. Lisa's apartment. Evening.

Video image, a scene from the video that LISA has taken out. LISA spots LANCE in the background of the shot and puts the VCR on pause. She stares at the frozen image, as the camera slowly zooms onto LANCE.

25. Interior. Hotel. Clara's room. Evening.

CLARA is looking through some photographs. She has placed a word processor beside her photograph of CLARENCE on the desk. CLARENCE shares some of LANCE's facial characteristics. As CLARA looks at the photo there is a brief flash of CLARENCE on video.

26. Interior. Cloud Nine video store. Evening.

LISA returns the videotape to the store. She drops it on the counter, and begins to leave.

> EDDY
> How did you like it?

LISA stops in her tracks. EDDY has never spoken to her before.

> LISA
> It was okay.

> EDDY
> You can keep it overnight. Most
> people do.

LISA *doesn't respond.* EDDY *picks up the tape, looks at it.*

> EDDY
>
> It's only partially wound.

LISA *doesn't respond.*

> EDDY
>
> They bore you?

> LISA
>
> No.

> EDDY
>
> Then what's the problem?

> LISA
>
> There isn't a problem.

> EDDY
>
> You always bring them back like this.
> I mean I can usually figure people
> out. I try to build up a character pro-
> file, watching what customers take
> out. But the thing about you is,
> there's no consistency.

EDDY *moves to a computer, and punches* LISA*'s file up on the screen.*

> EDDY
>
> I mean, look at these titles. You got
> horror, drama, comedy, even a bit of
> porn. And you've taken most of these
> out at least twenty times.

LISA *pauses, assessing the situation. She returns to the counter and slowly ex-*
tracts the eight-by-ten publicity photograph of LANCE *from her jacket. On the*
back of this glossy photograph is a résumé.

Screenplay

> LISA
> *(pointing to the résumé)*
> This is my lover.

> EDDY
> Ya?

> LISA
> He's an actor.

EDDY *takes the crumpled photograph from* LISA. *He stares at it.*

> LISA
> That's a list of movies he's been in.

EDDY *checks the movies on the résumé with those on his computer screen.*

> LISA
> I like to watch his scenes.

> EDDY
> Uh-huh. So he's your …?

> LISA
> He's my lover. I'm in love.

> EDDY
> What about him?

> LISA
> *(staring at* EDDY)
> You don't believe me.

> EDDY
> I didn't say that.

> LISA
> We work at the same place. A hotel.
> That's his day job.

EDDY

And he does his acting at night?

LISA

And days off. Sometimes he calls in
sick.

EDDY

He sounds dedicated.

LISA

He is.

EDDY *looks back at the résumé.*

EDDY

But he's just an extra.

LISA

What do you mean?

EDDY

Well, he may be in these movies, but
he doesn't have a speaking part.

LISA *stares at* EDDY.

EDDY

He doesn't talk in them.

LISA

He's on screen.

EDDY *smiles.* LISA *reaches for the photo-résumé and takes it back.*

LISA

There's nothing special about words.

LISA *begins to walk away.* EDDY *watches her leave.*

Screenplay   **27. Interior. Hotel. Housekeeper's office. Day.**

LANCE *is meeting with the* HOUSEKEEPER *of the hotel. The* HOUSE-
KEEPER *is an extremely well-kept woman in her mid-forties. Her* ASSISTANT
is a young man who looks similar to LANCE.

> HOUSEKEEPER
> And then, there are those who com-
> plain that you're not vocal enough.
> I'm not talking about noises here, or
> anything crude. It's just that some
> people thrive on compliments. And,
> ultimately, that's what we're all here
> to do. Compliment our guests while
> they stay with us.

The HOUSEKEEPER *smiles at* LANCE. *He turns his head away momentarily.*

> HOUSEKEEPER
> Now, I have a friend coming in at two.

> LANCE
> A good friend?

> HOUSEKEEPER
> Oh, I think you'll find this friend
> very good.

> LANCE
> *(smiles)*
> Alright.

> HOUSEKEEPER
> How are things with Lisa?

> LANCE
> Fine.

> HOUSEKEEPER
> Is she still bothering you?

Housekeeper moves into the frame.

26) INTERIOR. HOTEL. HOUSEKEEPER'S OFFICE. DAY.

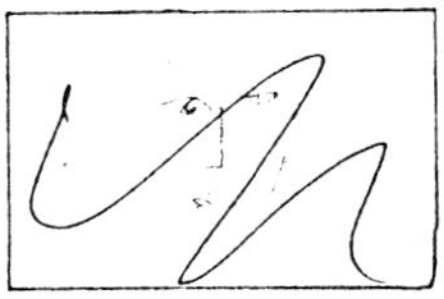

LANCE in a meeting with the HOUSEKEEPER of the hotel. The HOUSEKEEPER is an extremely well-kept woman in her mid-forties.

HOUSEKEEPER
I have a friend coming in at two.

LANCE
A good friend?

HOUSEKEEPER
This friend is very good.

LANCE (smiling)
Alright.

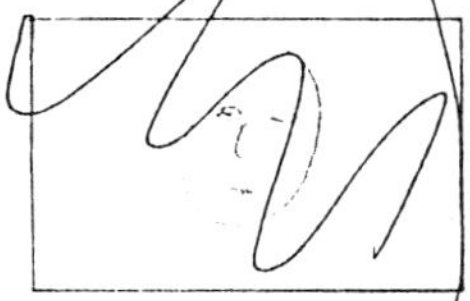

SU. Dolly Toy from keys to Housekeeper.

HOUSEKEEPER
How are things with Lisa?

LANCE
Fine.

HOUSEKEEPER
Is she still bothering you?

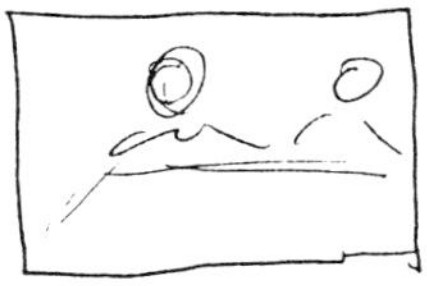

LANCE
Not really.

HOUSEKEEPER
I can have her let go. Find some excuse.

LANCE
It's not worth it.

HOUSEKEEPER
Or keep you separated. Make sure she's off your floor.

LANCE
Okay.

The HOUSEKEEPER smiles at LANCE.

CUT TO:

There was one person who thought you were speaking too much.

Rewrite

start on Lance slowly pull out of focus onto blurry frame, which reaches onto HOUSEKEEPER

SU1

HOUSEKEEPER
And then, of course, there are those who complain that you're not vocal enough. And I'm not referring to noises here. ~~[scribbled]~~ anything crude. It's just ~~that these are those who~~ some people thrive on compliments. And ultimately, that's what we're all here to do. Compliment our guests' ~~time with us.~~ while they're here with us.

The HOUSEKEEPER smiles at LANCE. He nods.

HOUSEKEEPER
Good. Now, I have a friend coming in at two.

LANCE
A good friend?

SU2

LANCE

HOUSEKEEPER
Oh, I think you'll find this friend very good.

LANCE
Alright.

LANCE stands.

HOUSEKEEPER
How are things with Lisa?

LANCE
Fine.

HOUSEKEEPER
Is she still bothering you?

SU3

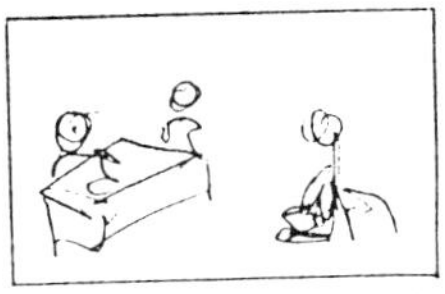

LANCE
Not really.

HOUSEKEEPER
I can have her let go. Find some excuse.

LANCE
It's not worth it.

Screenplay

> LANCE
>
> Not really.

> HOUSEKEEPER
>
> I could have her let go. Find some
> excuse.

> LANCE
>
> *(looks away again)*
>
> It's not worth it.

28. Interior. Hotel. Basement. Day.

LISA *is cleaning a wall in the hotel basement.*

29. Interior. Hotel. Clara's room. Day.

LANCE *goes to* CLARA*'s room to clean it. He notices the word processor, and a script beside it.* LANCE *leafs through the script.*

30. Interior. Hotel. Conference room. Day.

A tele-conference between CLARA *and the* PRODUCER *of the script that* LANCE *has discovered in* CLARA*'s room. The* PRODUCER *appears on a large video screen. He is thousands of miles away. There are a number of other people sitting around the long table in the conference room with* CLARA*, all of them associated with the production that the* PRODUCER *is orchestrating.*

> PRODUCER
>
> It's not difficult to make each other's
> lives more complicated, Clara.

> CLARA
>
> That's not what I'm saying.

> PRODUCER
>
> It's what you're doing.

CLARA *gestures to some of the other people in the room with her.*

> CLARA
>
> They've already started casting.

PRODUCER

Nothing's been finalized. You can
make any suggestions you want.
We're here to complement each
other's efforts. That's why I sent you
up there. To become more involved.
To help.

CLARA

How?

PRODUCER

Any way you want. If there's a location you see, if there's someone you
want to audition … feel free. We're
all working together on this. Okay?

Pause. CLARA *nods.*

PRODUCER

Good. So, how do you like the hotel?

CLARA

It's fine.

PRODUCER

Didn't I tell you. It's very special. So
… intimate.

31. Interior. Hotel. Hallway. Day.

LANCE *slips a manila envelope under the door of* CLARA*'s room, then walks
away down the hall.* CLARA *enters from another hallway and sees* LANCE
walking away.

32. Interior. Hotel. Clara's room. Day.

CLARA *enters her room to find the manila envelope under the door. She moves
to her desk and opens the envelope. She extracts the publicity photograph of*
LANCE. *She stares at it for a few moments, then turns to look at the photograph
of* CLARENCE. *She is struck by the similarity between the two faces. There is
a brief flash of* CLARENCE *on video.*

Screenplay   **33. Interior. Cloud Nine video store. Early evening.**

LISA and EDDY stand in one of the aisles in the store. She watches him as he casually returns tapes to their places on the shelves. EDDY hands LISA a tape.

EDDY
This one gets taken out a lot.

LISA
Is it any good?

EDDY
I wouldn't be able to tell you.

LISA
Why not?

EDDY
I never watch these things.

LISA
Then how do you know what to recommend?

EDDY
Well I don't. People check out the covers and take what they want.

LISA
Do you like working here?

EDDY
Not this part.

Pause.

LISA
What other part is there?

EDDY
Well, we rent equipment out.

LISA

What for?

EDDY

People want things recorded. Parties, weddings. The usual. And the not so usual. Sometimes I do it for them.

34. Interior. Hotel. Conference room. Early evening.

CLARA *is in the process of auditioning* LANCE. *They are alone. The audition is being videotaped.*

CLARA

Is this how you usually get auditions? Slipping your picture under some stranger's door?

LANCE

Well, I don't have an agent.

CLARA

Then how did you get in touch?

LANCE

I work at the hotel. Part-time. As a … consultant.

CLARA

What do you do?

LANCE

I help to book entertainment.

CLARA

So how do you know who I am?

LANCE

Well, I don't … exactly, I mean, I know you're involved with movies. I get a list of names of people in the

Screenplay

entertainment field that are staying
at the hotel. But I don't know exactly
what it is that you do.

CLARA
I could be a secretary.

Pause.

LANCE
Then why would you be doing this?

CLARA *stares at* LANCE. *She is smiling.*

CLARA
I can think of reasons.

Pause. LANCE *shifts uncomfortably in his seat.*

CLARA
Well, I'm not a secretary.

LANCE
(nervous laugh)
That's good.

CLARA
So, let's start. I'll read with you. If
you could look into the camera?

LANCE
Sure.

35. Interior. Cloud Nine video store. Storage area. Early evening.
*The storage area of the video store is a mess of monitors, boxes and various bits
of equipment. It is here that* EDDY *edits the material that he shoots for his
customers. Video images of a party: the image of a man sitting down in a chair
talking to someone. Angle on* EDDY, *showing* LISA *a tape he has made of a
wedding.* LISA *is fascinated by what she sees.*

LISA

How do you know what to film?

EDDY

You don't. You just go in there with your camera and get whatever you can.

LISA

What's happening here?

EDDY

Oh, I usually try to find a room where I can take people and get them to talk. This is the bride's dad.

The camera moves back to the video screen. EDDY *'s voice is heard off-screen, asking questions of the bride's* FATHER.

EDDY

Everyone's having a great time.

FATHER

Thank you.

EDDY

Is she your only daughter?

The FATHER *nods.* LISA *watches the video closely.*

EDDY

You've enjoyed a lot of applause in your career, but something extra-ordinarily dramatic is happening to you today. Can you give us any in-dication — and I know this is not the best time to ask — but what's going through your mind?

The FATHER *is speechless.*

Screenplay

> EDDY
> This must be a very happy day for
> you.

Angle on LISA *and* EDDY *watching the monitor.*

> EDDY
> *(off-screen)*
> I can honestly say that this is the best
> wedding I've ever taped.

LISA *turns to ask* EDDY *a question.*

> LISA
> Is that true?

> EDDY
> Of course not. You've seen one,
> you've seen 'em all.

36. Interior. Hotel. Conference room. Early evening.

LANCE *reads his audition piece with* CLARA. *He looks straight at the camera.*

> LANCE
> *(reading from the script)*
> There's nothing to be scared of.
> They've done this sort of operation
> before.

> CLARA
> *(also reading from the script)*
> I couldn't forgive myself if anything
> happened to you.

> LANCE
> Why should anything go wrong?

> CLARA
> The doctor said …

LANCE

There's a risk. That's all. And it's a
risk I have to take. You're my sister.
I'm not going to watch you die.

LANCE *finishes. He continues to look into the camera for a few moments, then*
turns to CLARA. *An angle on* CLARA *reveals that she is quite shaken by the*
reading.

LANCE

Okay?

CLARA

Yes.

LANCE

How was it?

CLARA

Fine.

LANCE

Do you want me to read it again?

CLARA

Alright.

LANCE

I have a question.

CLARA

Yes?

LANCE

Do I find out that you're dying in this
scene?

CLARA *stares at* LANCE. *She looks totally lost.*

Screenplay

> CLARA
>
> What?

> LANCE
>
> Is this the scene where I find out that
> you're dying?

> CLARA
>
> No. No. You found out before.

LANCE *nods and* CLARA *smiles.*

37. Interior. Cloud Nine video store. Storage area. Early evening.
Video image of the bride's FATHER *as he continues his interview with* EDDY.

> FATHER
>
> I'd do anything in the world to make
> her happy.

> EDDY
> *(off-screen)*
> Well, I think you have.

> FATHER
>
> Thank you.

Angle on LISA *and* EDDY *watching the monitor.*

> EDDY
> *(off-screen)*
> And now she's leaving the nest, about
> to embark on a new life. And let me
> tell you, she'll never forget this.

Video image of the FATHER. EDDY*'s last comment has had the desired effect.
The* FATHER *begins to dab at a tear with a handkerchief.* EDDY*'s camera
zooms in to get this action in close-up.*

> LISA
>
> It's amazing.

                              EDDY
What?

                              LISA
That you got him to do that.

                              EDDY
It's not too difficult. You've just got
to know what buttons to push.

38. Interior. Hotel. Conference room. Evening.
CLARA *and* LANCE *continue their audition.* CLARA *stares at* LANCE. *She
is almost in tears.* LANCE *is uncomfortable.*

                              LANCE
                      (reading from the script)
You don't have to say a word. It's good
to see you.

Pause.

                              LANCE
Was that any better? I can try it again.

                              CLARA
What do you think of the script?

                              LANCE
I like it.

                              CLARA
Really?

                              LANCE
Sure. I mean, it's a bit …

                              CLARA
Yes?

Screenplay

> LANCE
>
> Well, I had a little difficulty ...

> CLARA
>
> Believing it?

LANCE *nods.*

> CLARA
>
> It's all true.

39. Interior. Cloud Nine video store. Storage area. Evening.
LISA *implores* EDDY *as he rewinds the wedding tape.*

> LISA
>
> Please, Eddy.

> EDDY
>
> Look, it's not that easy.

> LISA
>
> I'll just watch. You don't have to pay
> me or anything. I'll help you move
> stuff round.

> EDDY
>
> But you just said you wanted to in-
> terview people.

> LISA
>
> If you think I can. I mean, I'll do
> whatever you want me to.

> EDDY
>
> Let me think about it.

> LISA
>
> Please.

40. Interior. Hotel. Conference room. Evening.

CLARA *and* LANCE *are wrapping up their audition.*

> LANCE
>
> I don't know if I should ask this, but … do you think I might have a chance?

> CLARA
>
> It's not up to me.

> LANCE
>
> Oh.

> CLARA
>
> Would this be your first speaking part?

> LANCE
>
> On film … yes. I mean, I've done some theatre. Nothing too big.

Beat. CLARA *turns to face* LANCE.

> CLARA
>
> So what *do* you do?

> LANCE
>
> Like I said, I work at the hotel.

> CLARA
>
> Part-time?

> LANCE
>
> No …

> CLARA
>
> Full-time?

Screenplay

                      LANCE
Yes.

                      CLARA
As an 'entertainment consultant' …?

LANCE *smiles. Pause.*

                      LANCE
I work in housekeeping.

                      CLARA
Ah …

                      LANCE
I was cleaning your room, and I saw
the script.

                      CLARA
So you took a chance.

                      LANCE
Yes.

                      CLARA
Do you do that often?

                      LANCE
What?

                      CLARA
Take chances.

LANCE *smiles at* CLARA. *There is a strong sexual tension between them.*

                      LANCE
Sometimes.

                      CLARA
When they're interesting.

Screenplay

Pause. They both smile sensually at each other.

41. **Interior. Hotel. Laundry room. Day.**
    The following morning. LISA *punches her card through the time-clock.*

42. **Interior. Hotel. Clara's room. Day.**
    LANCE *is asleep in bed.* CLARA *has left for a meeting.*

43. **Interior. Hotel. Laundry room. Day.**
    LISA *heads out of the laundry room with her loaded cart to make the first delivery of the day to the maids upstairs.*

44. **Interior. Hotel. Clara's room. Day.**
    LANCE *begins to wake up, then panics as he realizes where he is and what time it is.*

45. **Interior. Hotel. Hallway. Day.**
    LISA *is pushing her cart along one of the hallways upstairs.*

46. **Interior. Hotel. Clara's room. Day.**
    LANCE *dresses quickly.*

47. **Interior. Hotel. Hallway. Day.**
    LISA *approaches* CLARA*'s room.* LANCE *emerges from the room.* LISA *spots him.*

LISA

Lance?

LISA *chases after* LANCE, *who ignores* LISA *and runs down the hallway.*

LISA

Lance?

LANCE *ignores* LISA.

LISA

Lance!

LANCE *leaps into the elevator just as the door closes.* LISA *arrives too late and knocks against the closed elevator door.*

> LISA
>
> Lance!?!

48. Interior. Hotel. Conference room. Day.

The production team is seated around the long table, watching the wall monitor. CLARA *is playing with her pen. She looks up to see* CLARENCE *smiling at her from across the room. This shot of* CLARENCE *is on video, and is recognizable from the montage at the mausoleum at the beginning of the film.*

49. Interior. Hotel. Elevator. Day.

LANCE *shakes his head slowly, left to right.*

50. Interior. Hotel. Hallway. Day.

LISA *rubs her hands in a highly agitated manner as she moves down the hall.*

51. Interior. Hotel. Changing room. Day.

LANCE *races into the changing room. He puts his clothing into his locker. He has a print of his publicity photograph taped to the door.*

52. Interior. Hotel. Conference room. Day.

Close-up of CLARENCE *staring at* CLARA. *Again, this image is seen in video and seems to be totally out of context with the environment.*

53. Interior. Hotel. Conference room. Day.

Close-up of CLARA. *She is broken out of her daydream by the* PRODUCER's *voice.*

> PRODUCER
> *(off-screen)*
>
> Clara.

CLARA *looks up to the* PRODUCER's *image on the video monitor.*

> PRODUCER
>
> Clara.

Screenplay

54. Interior. Hotel. Changing room. Day.

LANCE *is dressing in front of a mirror.*

55. Interior. Hotel. Laundry room. Day.

LISA *is sorting laundry. She is upset about* LANCE.

56. Interior. Hotel. Housekeeper's office. Day.

The HOUSEKEEPER *is talking with her* ASSISTANT.

> HOUSEKEEPER
>
> I wouldn't see everyone. I mean, what time do you think would be allowable? For instance, from three o'clock until … three forty-four? Think so?

> ASSISTANT
>
> Yes. Definitely.

LANCE *rushes into the* HOUSEKEEPER'*s office and sits down.*

> HOUSEKEEPER
>
> You're very late, Lance.

> LANCE
>
> I'm sorry.

> HOUSEKEEPER
>
> We thought you might have deserted us.

> LANCE
>
> I wouldn't do that.

> HOUSEKEEPER
>
> I would like to think that this is an ideal working environment for you.

> LANCE
>
> It is.

HOUSEKEEPER
Good. How did you like my friend
in 106?

LANCE *manages a smile.*

HOUSEKEEPER
The feeling was mutual. I've cir-
cled in another appointment for
this afternoon.

LANCE
What time?

HOUSEKEEPER
During your work hours. Why?

LANCE
It's just that ... *(long pause)* I might
have to leave a bit early.

HOUSEKEEPER
I'm sure we can be flexible. My friend
was very taken with you.

LANCE
Alright.

HOUSEKEEPER
Do be careful though.

LANCE
What do you mean?

HOUSEKEEPER
This friend was quite smitten.
Remember what I told you about
distance. Cool mind. Cool heart.
Very playful body.

Screenplay

LANCE *smiles at the* HOUSEKEEPER.

57. Interior. Hotel. Conference room. Day.

A tele-conference with the production team. The central figure in this meeting is the PRODUCER *of the television show, who appears on the video monitor. He is watching* LANCE*'s audition piece on a smaller monitor on the conference table.*

> LANCE
> *(reading)*
> This is not an everyday sort of a sit-
> uation, Julie. You could be dying.
> Besides, your fear isn't justified. I've
> talked to the doctor. There's nothing
> to be scared of. They've done this
> sort of operation before ...

The PRODUCER *turns to face* CLARA. *She stares at* LANCE*'s image.*

> LANCE
> *(off-screen)*
> ... it's a matter of my feeling to you.
> You can't expect me not to react to
> this in what would normally be con-
> sidered an extreme manner ...

> PRODUCER
> *(off-screen)*
> You're sure?

> CLARA
> Yes.

> PRODUCER
> He's what you're looking for?

> CLARA
> Exactly.

> PRODUCER
> You find him natural enough?

CLARA *nods.*

PRODUCER

Well, let's think about it. We have a few more days.

CLARA

He's my choice.

PRODUCER

And I respect that. Now, did you get my revisions?

CLARA

Yes.

PRODUCER

And how did you feel about them?

CLARA

They're unacceptable. I hate the idea of putting in the talk show. It doesn't add anything.

PRODUCER

Well, it's a unique way of getting the information across. Nothing's more boring than people in a doctor's office, discussing the disease of the week.

CLARA

But it cheapens the point.

PRODUCER

What 'point'? This isn't one of your university lectures, Clara. You're not in a classroom anymore. We're not presenting a thesis. We're telling a story.

Screenplay

CLARA

My story.

The PRODUCER *stares at* CLARA *from the monitor. Undaunted, she stares back.*

PRODUCER

Look, this isn't the time to argue.

CLARA

When is?

PRODUCER

When I'm less busy.

CLARA

You're never less busy.

PRODUCER

I can't talk like this.

CLARA

Alright. I'll come there.

The PRODUCER *continues to stare at* CLARA.

58. Interior. Hotel. Guest room. Day.

LANCE *is buttoning up his shirt in one of the rooms. There is someone taking a shower in the washroom. A figure can be made out through the curtain, though it is impossible to tell if it is male or female.* LANCE *leaves the room.*

59. Interior. Hotel. Hallway. Day.

LANCE *is moving down the hall, away from Room 106. He turns the corner and discovers* CLARA *leaving her room.* CLARA *is taking her suitcase with her.* LANCE *stops to talk to* CLARA.

CLARA

Hi.

LANCE

Where are you going?

92

                    CLARA
I have to go back.

                    LANCE
Why?

                    CLARA
Complications. I'm sorry I had to
leave so early this morning.

                    LANCE
That's okay.

                    LANCE
Are you returning?

                    CLARA
I'm not sure.

                    LANCE
Do we stay in touch?

                    CLARA
Over what?

Pause. LANCE *leans forward and kisses* CLARA.

                    LANCE
Us.

CLARA *gazes at* LANCE.

                    CLARA
We can still see each other.

                    LANCE
How?

60. Interior. Hotel. Laundry room. Day.
    LISA *is mopping the floor. She stops, drinks from a cup.*

57) INTERIOR. HOTEL. STAFF CAFETERIA. DAY.

LANCE in the staff cafeteria, sitting by himself at a table.
LISA appears out of nowhere and sits down beside him.

                    LISA
          Lance, what's going on?

Pause. LANCE ignores LISA's presence.

                    LISA
          I know how upset you get.

LANCE ignores LISA.

                    LISA
          I know how special you are. You
          can't let other people make you feel
          small.

LANCE ignores LISA.

                    LISA
          Let me love you.

The camera ducks underneath the table to reveal LISA's hand
finding it's way to LANCE's crotch, which she tries to massage.
LANCE's hand grabs hers, and pulls LISA's hand back to the table.
The focus resolves onto the HOUSEKEEPER watching this scene in
the background.

Handwritten annotations:

You don't have the right to make other people feel this way.

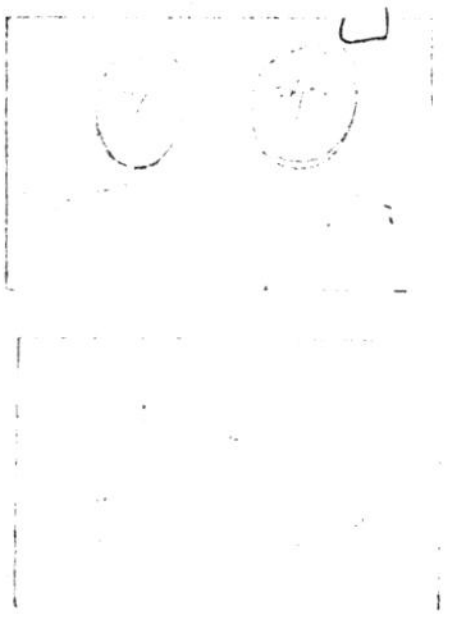

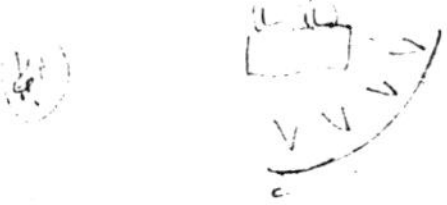

What are you being made to feel?

You're very

I know you're ~~think~~ a r thinking about me. I know

I know that you're thinking about me

I know that you thin SUBTEXT

Kenker—
I know that you thin SUBTEXT

I ~~know That~~ our relationship

I know that other people can't understand me.
I know that you can.

I know that you can feel me feeling you. That's why you can't really ignore me.

I know that it bothers you to act like this; to pretend that I'm not here. I think I understand why you have to do it.

But Lance, don't let other people make you feel small. I know how special you are.
Let me love you.

58) EXTERIOR. VIDEO STORE. EVENING.

Outside the video store, later that evening. LISA enters the
frame, and finds her way to the entrance of the store.

cut?

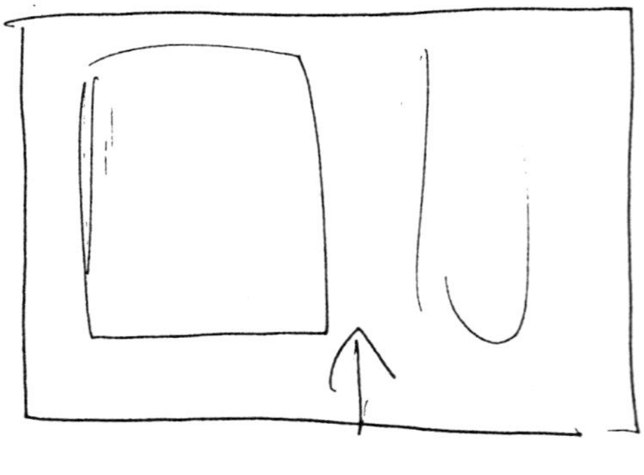

61. Interior. Hotel. Staff cafeteria. Day.

LANCE *in the staff cafeteria, sitting by himself at a table.* LISA *appears out of nowhere and sits down beside him.*

LISA

Lance, what's going on?

Pause. LANCE *ignores* LISA*'s presence.*

LISA

I know how upset you get.

LANCE *ignores* LISA.

LISA

You're very special. You can't let other
people make you feel small.

LANCE *ignores* LISA.

LISA

Let me love you.

LISA*'s hand reaches under the table, finding its way to* LANCE*'s crotch, which she tries to massage.* LANCE*'s hand takes hers, and pulls it back to the table.* LANCE *gets up and leaves, revealing the* HOUSEKEEPER, *who has been watching this scene, in the background.* LISA *turns to stare at the* HOUSEKEEPER.

62. Interior. Hotel. Housekeeper's office. Day.

LISA *is seated opposite the* HOUSEKEEPER. *Her* ASSISTANT *is placing keys onto a board in the background.*

HOUSEKEEPER

You see, there's a side of me that sees you all as children. My children. I don't mean that in a negative way. I am concerned about your well-being, and making this as comfortable a working environment as possible. If you accept this notion,

Screenplay

then it's not too difficult to understand why I would have favourites. And, some children are naturally more lovable. Others ... well, others have to work harder at gaining the attention they feel they deserve. Does that answer your question?

LISA *nods her head.*

63. Exterior. Cloud Nine video store. Evening.
Outside the video store, later that evening. LISA *enters the frame, and makes her way to the entrance of the store.*

64. Interior. Cloud Nine video store. Evening.
LISA *approaches the counter of the store.* EDDY *is not there. She approaches a* CLERK *in one of the aisles.*

LISA

Is Eddy here?

CLERK

No.

LISA

Where is he?

CLERK

Shooting a party.

LISA

Where is the party?

CLERK

Why?

LISA

He wanted me to help him.

The CLERK *looks at* LISA *suspiciously.*

CLERK

To help him do what?

LISA

Help him tape it.

65. Interior. Hotel. Hallway. Evening.

LANCE *walks down a darkened staircase and crosses a darkened foyer in the conference section of the hotel. He arrives at the door of the tele-conference room. Using the master key, of which he has procured a copy, he opens the door of this room. He closes the door, then turns on the lights to the room. He walks over to the conference table and takes a seat at the head of the table.*

66. Interior. Warehouse building. Evening.

LISA *walks up a flight of stairs. Loud party music can be heard. She approaches a man guarding the door.*

GUARD

Ya?

LISA

Is Eddy here?

GUARD

Who?

LISA

Eddy. I think he's taping the party.

The GUARD *nods and allows* LISA *inside, taking a Polaroid of her as she enters the room. People are wandering around the room. Raucous dance music plays. The atmosphere of an orgy.*

67. Interior. Hotel. Conference room. Evening.

LANCE *sits in the room, waiting for* CLARA *to appear on the screen. He takes off his jacket. After a moment,* CLARA *appears.*

CLARA

Hello.

Screenplay

> LANCE
> *(laughs)*
>
> Hi.

> CLARA
>
> How are you?

> LANCE
>
> Fine.

> CLARA
>
> I hope this isn't too strange for you.

> LANCE
>
> No. *(he laughs)* Did you have a good trip?

> CLARA
>
> Fine.

> LANCE
>
> When did you get in?

> CLARA
>
> A couple of hours ago.

Pause.

> LANCE
>
> I missed you.

> CLARA
>
> Really?

> LANCE
>
> Yes.

LANCE *and* CLARA *stare at each other on the screens.*

su 1, 2, 3

Field 3

F 1

Field 2

63) INTERIOR. HOTEL. CONFERENCE ROOM. EVENING.

The tele-conference room. LANCE and CLARA face each other on the
video screens. They stare at each other without speaking a word.
Both are partially undressed, and are playing with themselves.
After a moment, CLARA begins to laugh. LANCE begins to laugh as
well. The laughter dies down.

                         CLARA
         I watched your audition again today.
                         LANCE
         And?
                         CLARA
         It's very good.
                         LANCE
         You mean that...?
                         CLARA
         You might have a chance.

LANCE can't believe this news. CLARA begins to zip up her dress
as she smiles at LANCE.

CLARA: hand massages
breast as she
masturbates herself

the film camera
scans over this
video image

su 4

Both Clara +
Lance's eyes
are closed.
MINIMUM NOISE

NO GRUNTS, MOANS, etc

LANCE's
penis is
framed out
by table.

su. 5

image of
Clara reflected
in mirror
door.

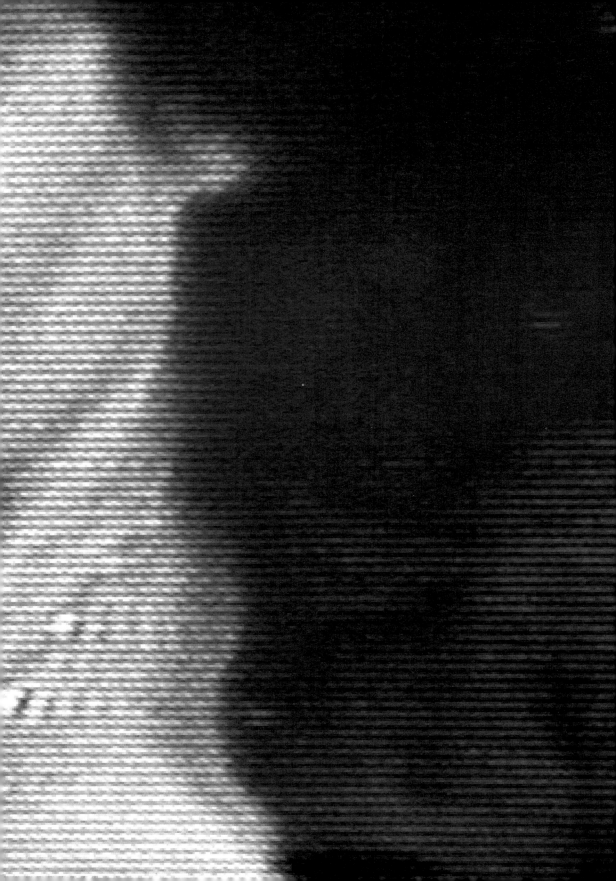

Screenplay

68. Interior. Warehouse loft. Evening.

LISA *walks through the party. People are undressed and coupling. A clothed couple holds hands. They smile expectantly.* LISA *approaches* EDDY *as he tapes two women embracing.*

69. Interior. Hotel. Conference room. Evening.

The tele-conference room. LANCE *and* CLARA *face each other on the video screens. They stare at each other without speaking a word. Both are partially undressed and are masturbating. When* CLARA *has an orgasm they stop and smile at each other.* LANCE *stretches out his leg, which has been resting on the table top, and breaks a table lamp.* CLARA *begins to laugh.* LANCE *begins to laugh as well. The laughter dies down.*

> CLARA
> I watched your audition again today.

> LANCE
> And?

> CLARA
> It's very good.

70. Interior. Warehouse loft. Evening.

LISA *stands behind* EDDY.

> EDDY
> What are you doing here?

> LISA
> I came to see if you needed any help.

> EDDY
> No.

> LISA
> Eddy, why are you doing this?

> EDDY
> Because it's part of my job.

> LISA

But it's ...

> EDDY

Look, we'll talk about this later.
Come by the store tomorrow. Okay?

LISA *nods, and, staring at the spectacle one last time, leaves the room. She is deeply disturbed by what she has witnessed.*

71. Interior. Hotel. Guest room. Evening.

LANCE *is sitting in a guest's room. He dusts lazily, then he starts to vacuum.*

72. Interior. Hotel. Laundry room. Evening.

LISA *works at the laundry press.*

73. Interior. Hotel. Changing room. Evening.

LANCE *shaves in front of a mirror.*

74. Interior. Hotel. Basement. Evening.

LISA *carries laundry down a basement hallway.*

75. Interior. Hotel. Conference room. Evening.

LANCE *sits smoking, waiting for* CLARA *to appear on the screen. She does.*

> CLARA

Hi there.

> LANCE

Hello.

> CLARA

How was your day?

> LANCE

Alright.

> CLARA

What happened?

Screenplay

LANCE

Not much. How are things on your
end?

CLARA

Not too good.

76. Interior. Hotel. Hallway. Evening.

LISA *is working the night shift. She is delivering some extra towels to Room 106. She knocks on the door.*

77. Interior. Hotel. Guest room. Evening.

This is the room that the HOUSEKEEPER's *'friend' is staying in. There is no response to the knock.* LISA *enters the dark room.*

LISA

Housekeeping.

The lights in the washroom are on. LISA *pauses outside the washroom door.*

LISA

Housekeeping.

Pause.

LISA

You ordered some extra towels.

No response. A person's soft sobs are heard emanating from the washroom.

LISA

I'll just leave them on the counter.

Pause. LISA *waits for a moment, rests the towels on the counter, then leaves the room.*

78. Interior. Hotel. Conference room. Evening.

CLARA *and* LANCE *continue their conversation.*

CLARA

I'm not the casting director.

LANCE

What do you mean?

CLARA

I'm the writer.

Pause.

CLARA

I was told that I'd have input over casting. That's why I auditioned you. They liked your audition, by the way. You might have the part.

LANCE *is overwhelmed by this possibility.*

CLARA

You won't find out for a couple of days. But you could find out sooner, if you want.

LANCE

How?

CLARA

The producer's assistant is staying in the room next to mine. That's where all the casting information is kept. You can sneak in there tomorrow night.

LANCE

Sneak in?

CLARA

One of the producer's friends is

Screenplay

getting married. Everyone will be at the wedding.

> LANCE
> Are you sure?

> CLARA
> Positive.

Pause.

> CLARA
> When you're inside the room, I want you to do me a favour.

Pause.

> CLARA
> I want you to find a copy of the revised script. It'll be printed on pink paper. Is that clear?

> LANCE
> Don't you have a copy?

> CLARA
> Why would I?

> LANCE
> Well, if you're the writer ...

CLARA *begins to laugh.*

> LANCE
> What's so funny?

> CLARA
> I'm only the writer.

79. Interior. Hotel. Ballroom. Evening.

A lavish wedding party. The first guests that are seen at this event are recognizable from the tele-conference sessions at the hotel. They are CLARA*'s business colleagues.*

80. Interior. Hotel. Small room beside ballroom. Evening.

A small room close to the party. The sounds of the celebration are heard in this room, as EDDY *hangs a backdrop and* LISA *looks through the video camera.*

EDDY

Is that clear?

LISA

Yes.

EDDY

You're sure you know what you're doing?

LISA

Uh-huh.

EDDY

I just want an interview with the bride. That's all. Nothing fancy. Just get a sense of her excitement. Okay?

LISA

Yes.

EDDY

I'm trusting you here. These are very important people.

LISA

How did you get the job?

EDDY

I was personally recommended.

71) INTERIOR. HOTEL. BALLROOM. EVENING.

A lavish wedding party. The first guests that are seen at this event are recognized from the tele-conference sessions at the hotel. They are CLARA's business colleagues.

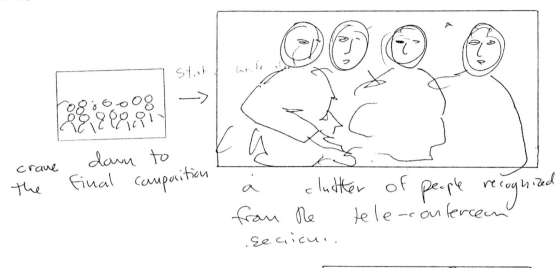

Start with...

craue down to the final composition

a clutter of people recognized fran the tele-conferean secicn.

72) INTERIOR. HOTEL. SMALL ROOM BESIDE BALLROOM. EVENING.

A small room close to the party. The sounds of the celebration are heard in this room, as EDDY shows LISA how to work the video camera.

SU.

Eddy sets up the screen, and mouel away on

I just want an interview.

SU 2

         EDDY
Is that clear?

         LISA
Yes.

         EDDY
You're sure you know what you're doing?

         LISA
Uh-huh.

         EDDY
I just want an interview with the bride. That's all. Nothing fancy. Just a get a sense of her excitement. Okay?

         LISA
Yes.

image conditions

         EDDY
I'm trusting you here. These are very important people.

         LISA
How did you get the job.

         EDDY
I was personally recommended.

81. Interior. Hotel. Hallway. Evening.

LANCE *moving down one of the hallways at the hotel, towards the room he will break into. He arrives at the door, and extracts the key from his pocket.*

82. Interior. Hotel. Ballroom. Evening.

LISA *is floating through the crowd at the party. There are a number of other people there also taping the event. She seems slightly dazed by the commotion. She talks to an older man, recognizable as the* FATHER *from the video in Scenes 35 and 37.*

LISA

Excuse me.

FATHER

Yes?

LISA

Are you related to the bride?

FATHER

Not this time.

LISA *stares at the* FATHER, *not sure of where she's seen him before.*

83. Interior. Hotel. Guest room. Evening.

LANCE *enters the guest room where the* PRODUCER*'s assistant is staying. He begins to look around.*

84. Interior. Hotel. Ballroom. Evening.

The FATHER *is leading* LISA *through the crowded party. Suddenly, on a large screen on one wall of the ballroom, a huge image of the* PRODUCER *is projected. All heads in the ballroom turn to regard this image.*

PRODUCER
(his image addresses the assembled mass)

Hello, everyone. I'm very sorry I couldn't be there to share this special evening with you.

Screenplay

As the PRODUCER *continues his speech, the* FATHER *points out the bride to* LISA.

> FATHER
>
> That's her.

The camera moves down to show the bride, TRISH — *an odd-looking woman who shares many of* LISA*'s odd features — and the groom,* RONNIE — *who bears more than a passing resemblance to* LANCE. *They are listening to the* PRODUCER.

> FATHER
>
> And that's the groom.

> PRODUCER
> *(continuing his speech)*
> Most of us gathered here tonight are
> in the profession of making fairy
> tales. But sometimes, these dreams
> come true, and that's certainly the
> case when two people as special as
> Ronnie and Trish get married.

The audience breaks into applause. The PRODUCER *also applauds.* RONNIE *and* TRISH *kiss.* LISA *stares at them from a distance.*

85. Interior. Hotel. Guest room. Evening.
LANCE *finds the revised script. He finds a videotape marked 'Final Choices.'* LANCE *takes the tape and script with him and leaves the room.*

86. Interior. Hotel. Small room beside ballroom. Evening.
Video image of RONNIE *and* TRISH. *The bride and groom are cuddling each other.*

> RONNIE
>
> And then I saw her in this little
> bikini. You remember?

TRISH *laughs. The camera moves to show* LISA *behind the video camera, and the bride and groom in front of the camera.*

> LISA
>
> Ron, I'm wondering if it might be possible to have a few moments alone with Trish.

> RONNIE
>
> What for?

> LISA
>
> I'd just like to ask her some questions.

> RONNIE
>
> About me?

RONNIE *and* TRISH *giggle hysterically over this notion.* LISA *waits for them to calm down.*

> LISA
>
> Would that be okay?

> RONNIE
>
> I guess so.

RONNIE *kisses* TRISH *and departs, leaving the bride staring rather vulnerably into* LISA*'s lens.*

87. Interior. Hotel. Conference room. Evening.

LANCE *is watching his audition on a small monitor inside the conference room.* CLARA *is also watching from the video screen in the room. His audition is audible and visible on the video monitor for the rest of the scene.*

> CLARA
>
> Congratulations.

> LANCE
>
> Are you sure that's what it means?

> CLARA
>
> Does it say 'Final Choices' on the tape?

Screenplay

LANCE

Yes.

CLARA

Then that's what they are.

Pause. LANCE *tries to absorb the significance of this.*

CLARA

Did you find a copy of the script?

LANCE
(holding up the document)

Here.

CLARA

Turn to page 73.

LANCE *turns the pink script to page 73.*

CLARA

Read me what it says.

88. Interior. Hotel. Small room beside ballroom. Evening.
Video image of the bride as she is being taped by LISA. LISA *looks through the camera at* TRISH.

LISA

Are you ready?

TRISH

I think so.

LISA

What do you see in Ronnie?

TRISH

What?

114

Screenplay

> LISA
>
> What do you see in Ronnie? When you look at him, what are you looking at?

> TRISH
> *(perplexed)*
>
> Him.

> LISA
>
> Did it come easy?

> TRISH
>
> What?

> LISA
>
> His love?

> TRISH
> *(giggling)*
>
> I'm not quite sure if I get what …

> LISA
>
> Have there been times when it didn't seem so … certain?

> TRISH
>
> No, I …

> LISA
>
> I mean, these things are pretty delicate, aren't they? There's no telling what could happen. One of you begins to have second thoughts and the whole thing can crumble away. And then what?

TRISH *stares, dumbfounded, into the camera.*

80) INTERIOR. HOTEL. SMALL ROOM BESIDE BALLROOM. EVENING.

Video image of the bride as she is being taped by LISA.

~~Crest of numberings~~

LISA
Are you ready?

TRISH
I think so.

LISA
What do you see in Ronnie?

TRISH
What?

What do you see _in_ Ronnie. (beat) When
you look at him, what are you looking _at_?

TRISH
Him.

LISA
Did it come easy?

TRISH
What?.....

LISA
His love?

TRISH
I'm not sure if I get what...

LISA
Have there been times when it didn't
seem so certain?

TRISH
No...

LISA
I mean, these things are pretty
delicate, aren't they? There's no
telling what could happen. One of
you begins to have second thoughts
and the whole thing can crumble away.
And then what?

TRISH stares dumbfoundedly into the camera.

dolly to:

LISA

what do you see in Ronnie?

TRISH
What?

LISA
~~what do you see in Trish?~~
what do you see in Ronnie?
When you look at him,
what you are you looking _at_?

TRISH
Him.

S.u. 1   Trish waiting   Lisa fiddles with camera "Are you ready?"

Lisa moves behind the
camera as the actor
moves, to isolate Trish
"How did you end up..."

At the camera

S.u. 2

④ ⓑ

Herman Furi
863 Bay & Grosvenor
Ontario Herbie Polly Review

MIKE

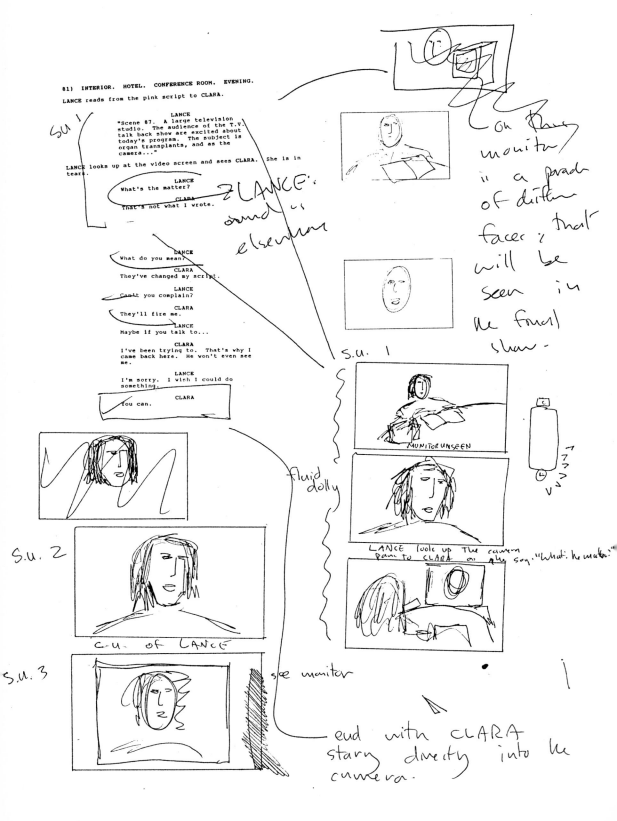

81) INTERIOR. HOTEL. CONFERENCE ROOM. EVENING.

LANCE reads from the pink script to CLARA.

S.u 1

LANCE
"Scene 87. A large television
studio. The audience of the T.V.
talk back show are excited about
today's program. The subject is
organ transplants, and as the
camera..."

LANCE looks up at the video screen and sees CLARA. She is in
tears.

LANCE:
What's the matter?

ZLANCE: oundis elsewhere

CLARA
That's not what I wrote.

LANCE
What do you mean?

CLARA
They've changed my script.

LANCE
Can't you complain?

CLARA
They'll fire me.

LANCE
Maybe if you talk to...

CLARA
I've been trying to. That's why I
came back here. He won't even see
me.

LANCE
I'm sorry. I wish I could do
something.

CLARA
You can.

On Pers monitor is a parade of differ faces; that will be seen in the final show.

S.u. 1

MONITOR UNSEEN

LANCE look up The camera pans to CLARA as she say. "What is the matter"

fluid dolly

S.u. 2

C.u. of LANCE

S.u. 3

s/e monitor

end with CLARA staring directly into the camera.

89. Interior. Hotel. Conference room. Evening.

LANCE *reads from the pink script to* CLARA. *His audition is still audible.*

> LANCE
>
> 'Scene 87. A large television studio. The audience of the TV talk-back show are excited about today's program. The subject is organ transplants, and as the camera ...'

LANCE *looks up at the video screen and sees* CLARA. *She is very upset.*

> LANCE
>
> What's the matter?

> CLARA
>
> That's not what I wrote.

> LANCE
>
> What do you mean?

> CLARA
>
> They've changed my script.

> LANCE
>
> Can't you complain?

> CLARA
>
> They'll fire me.

> LANCE
>
> Maybe if you talk to ...

> CLARA
>
> I'm trying to. That's why I came here. He won't even see me.

> LANCE
>
> I'm sorry. I wish I could do something.

Screenplay

Pause.

> CLARA
>
> You can.

90. Interior. Hotel. Small room beside ballroom. Evening.

TRISH *seems distressed. She and* LISA *gaze at each other.*

> TRISH
>
> Why would you ask me that?

> LISA
>
> Why not?

> TRISH
>
> I don't even know you.

> LISA
>
> *(this is spoken very fast)*
>
> It's just that these sort of questions interest me. I mean, love is about … feeling someone else feeling you, right? But sometimes, you can feel someone else, and you can feel them feeling you, but they may not act that way. In your case, it's the other way around. He says that he loves you, which is great, but I'm not sure if that matters. The question is, 'Do you feel him feeling you the way you feel yourself'?

> TRISH
>
> Why should I even think about it?

> LISA
>
> Because years from now, when you look back at this tape, your answer might be really … interesting.

The bride suddenly breaks down, and rushes out of the room.

>   LISA
> Hey, hey, come back.

91. Interior. Hotel. Conference room. Evening.
CLARA *explains her plan to* LANCE. *His audition is still audible.*

>   CLARA
> This script is very important.

>   LANCE
> You said before it was based on a true
> story.

>   CLARA
> It happened to me.

Pause.

>   CLARA
> And my brother.

>   LANCE
> So what can I do?

>   CLARA
> They'll cast you, and ... you'll meet
> the producer. He won't listen to me.
> He might listen to you.

>   LANCE
> Why?

>   CLARA
> Because you're an actor. You can sug-
> gest things you think your character
> might do.

Screenplay

>   LANCE
> And if he doesn't listen?
>
>   CLARA
> You can threaten to leave.
>
>   LANCE
> But I'm nothing to them, Clara.
>
>   CLARA
> Not until they start shooting. Then
> you're worth a lot. I mean, they can't
> cut you out, and they can't shoot
> everything over with someone else.
> Do you understand?

LANCE *nods.*

92. Interior. Hotel. Ballroom. Evening.

The groom, RONNIE, *is angrily confronting* EDDY. LISA *stands nearby.*

>   RONNIE
> Why is my wife in tears?
>
>   EDDY
> I'm sorry, I did not talk to your wife,
> I did not talk to your wife. I'm sorry.
> I'm going to think about this.

RONNIE *grabs* EDDY *by the collar of his shirt, ready to punish him for upsetting his wife.*

>   RONNIE
> I only know one thing —
>
>   EDDY
> Hey look, this had nothing to do
> with me.

EDDY *points at* LISA.

84) INTERIOR. HOTEL. BALLROOM. EVENING.

A huge crowd has gathered around LISA and EDDY. The groom,
RONNIE, is holding EDDY by the cuff of his shirt, ready to punish
him for upsetting his wife.

                    EDDY
          Look, this had nothing to do with me.
          She taped her.

EDDY points to LISA. RONNIE grabs LISA.

                              RONNIE
          Where is it?
                              LISA
          What?
                              RONNIE
          The tape!

Terrified, LISA points to the small room where she taped TRISH.

a huge crowd gathered around Eddy Ron and Lisa

A   BRAWL

she taped her!

EDDY

She taped her!

RONNIE *releases* EDDY *and turns to* LISA.

RONNIE

Where is it?

LISA

What?

RONNIE

The tape!

RONNIE *grabs* LISA *in a threatening manner. She gasps.*

93. Interior. Hotel. Conference room. Evening.

CLARA *and* LANCE *continue their conversation over the sound of* LANCE's
audition.

CLARA

Will you do it?

LANCE

I suppose so.

CLARA

You don't seem very enthusiastic.

LANCE

It's just that …

CLARA

Yes?

LANCE

This is a big chance for me.

CLARA

And you don't want to screw it up.

LANCE

(nods)

Yes.

CLARA

Doesn't what I'm going through
mean anything to you?

Pause.

CLARA

Do I have to beg?

LANCE

No.

94. Interior. Hotel. Small room beside ballroom. Evening.

RONNIE *enters to find* LISA. *He grabs the video camera (still attached to the tripod), and shoves the lens into* LISA*'s face.*

RONNIE

You like that?!

LISA

No.

RONNIE

What?

LISA

No!

RONNIE

Don't do it to other people!

RONNIE *throws the camera down and leaves the room.* LISA *is distraught.*

95. Interior. Hotel. Conference room. Evening.

CLARA *and* LANCE *end their conversation.*

Screenplay

> CLARA
>
> This is going to end pretty soon.

> LANCE
>
> What?

> CLARA
>
> The line. I only booked half an hour.

> LANCE
>
> Oh.

> CLARA
>
> You have my number. Call me any time.

> LANCE
>
> Okay.

> CLARA
>
> What are you thinking?

> LANCE
>
> Nothing.

Pause. They stare at one another.

> CLARA
>
> And Lance?

> LANCE
>
> Yes?

> CLARA
>
> Congratulations. You must be very excited.

> LANCE
>
> Yes, I …

87) INTERIOR. HOTEL. CONFERENCE ROOM. EVENING.

CLARA and LANCE end their conversation.

                    CLARA
          This is going to end pretty soon.
                    LANCE
          What?
                    CLARA
          The line. I only booked half an
          hour.
                    LANCE
          Oh.
                    CLARA
          You have my number. Call me any
          time.
                    LANCE
          Okay.
                    CLARA
          What are you thinking?
                    LANCE
          Nothing.
                    CLARA
          And Lance?
                    LANCE
          Yes?
                    CLARA
          Congratulations. You must be very
          excited.
                    LANCE
          Yes, I...

          The line is cut. CLARA's frozen image remains on the screen for
          a moment, then fades away. LANCE pauses for a moment, then rises
          from his seat and leaves the room, taking the tape and the script
          with him.

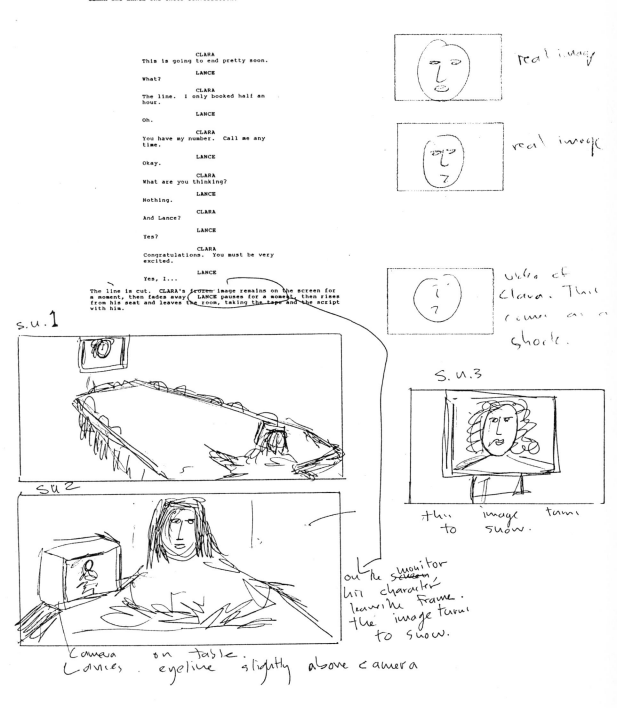

real image

real image

video of Clara. This comes as a shock.

s.u.1

su2

S.u.3

this image turns to snow.

on the monitor his character leaves the frame. the image turns to snow.

Camera on table. Lances eyeline slightly above camera

Screenplay   *The line is cut.* CLARA*'s frozen image remains on the screen for a moment, then fades away.* LANCE*'s audition tape stops simultaneously.* LANCE *pauses for a moment, then rises from his seat, about to leave the room.*

96. Interior. Hotel. Small room beside ballroom. Evening.
EDDY *enters the room and approaches* LISA*, who is sitting on the couch.*

> EDDY
> You okay?

LISA *is motionless.*

> EDDY
> Look, I'm sorry about pointing the
> finger at you.

LISA *nods slightly.*

> EDDY
> You see what I mean about it being
> a bit tricky?

> LISA
> I lost my objectivity.

> EDDY
> Well, that can happen.

> LISA
> It doesn't happen to you.

> EDDY
> Maybe it should.

Pause.

> EDDY
> Look, I gotta get back. Can you get
> home okay?

LISA
You don't want me around?

EDDY
I don't think it would be such a great
idea. I'll see you at the shop. Tomorrow. Okay?

LISA *nods.* EDDY *rises and leaves the room.* LISA *is deeply shaken.*

97. Exterior. Subway exit. Day.
LANCE *emerges from the subway exit and walks off.*

98. Interior. Hotel. Hallway. Day.
LISA *walks down one of the hallways in the hotel. Two ambulance attendants
carry the* HOUSEKEEPER's *friend on a stretcher out of the room* LISA *delivered the towels to two nights previously. She stops and stares as the body is
wheeled past her and down the hall.*

99. Interior. Hotel. Deluxe suite. Day.
The deluxe suite that the PRODUCER *is staying in.* LANCE *is meeting the*
PRODUCER *for the first time.*

PRODUCER
You're probably wondering how you
got the part.

LANCE
Well …

PRODUCER
Lance, I'd like you to meet Ronnie.

The PRODUCER *shows* LANCE *a picture of* RONNIE. *He is immediately recognizable as the groom from the wedding scene.*

PRODUCER
You might notice that you look like
Ronnie. That's because you'll be

Screenplay

playing his brother. He's the guy you give your lung to.

LANCE
I'm not sure I understand.

PRODUCER
The transplant. You've read the script. You give your lung to Ronnie.

LANCE
But I thought I gave it to my sister.

PRODUCER
There's been a change.

100. Interior. Hotel. Housekeeper's office. Day.
LISA *enters the* HOUSEKEEPER*'s office for questioning by an unseen officer. The* HOUSEKEEPER *is seated at the far end of the office. The questioning officer is identified only by her voice.*

VOICE
Please sit down, Lisa. We've had a suicide in Room 106. Were you aware of the person staying in that room? Did you have any contact with him?

LISA *nods.*

101. Interior. Hotel. Deluxe suite. Day.
The PRODUCER*'s hotel suite. The* PRODUCER *takes a contract from his briefcase and hands it to* LANCE. TRISH *is working at a computer.*

PRODUCER
Well, if you don't have any questions, Lance, I suppose we can think of signing this.

LANCE

Shouldn't I have someone look it over?

PRODUCER

I thought you didn't have an agent.

LANCE

I have a friend. A lawyer. I mean, if that's okay with you.

PRODUCER

Sure it's okay with me. As long as there aren't any problems.

LANCE

I'm sure there won't be any.

PRODUCER

When do you think we might have this settled?

LANCE

I'm meeting my friend tomorrow.

PRODUCER

Wednesday morning, then?

LANCE

Yes, that should be fine.

PRODUCER

I'll probably be out of town. But we can meet by conference. Upstairs. Trish will tell you about it.

LANCE

You must be busy.

Screenplay

PRODUCER

I'm shooting three of these suckers
right now. But this one's very special
to me.

102. Interior. Hotel. Housekeeper's office. Day.

LISA *is being questioned by an unseen officer. The* HOUSEKEEPER *is sitting behind* LISA.

VOICE

Do you know if any of our staff had
any contact with the guest? Did you
see anyone going into the room?
Coming out?

LISA

I don't think so.

VOICE

You're sure?

LISA *nods.*

VOICE

You said before that you heard someone crying when you delivered the
towels.

LISA

Yes.

VOICE

You don't think that they might have
been crying over someone like
Lance?

LISA

No.

                              VOICE
                  And you're positive about that?

LISA *nods.*

103. Interior. Subway station. Day.
LANCE reads a newspaper while waiting for a train.

104. Interior. Hotel. Housekeeper's office. Day.
The questioning comes to an end.

                              VOICE
                  Did Lance ever talk to you about re-
                  ceiving any 'gifts' from our guests?

LISA *turns to look at the* HOUSEKEEPER.

                         HOUSEKEEPER
                  Housekeeping staff do not receive
                  gratuities.

LISA *and the* HOUSEKEEPER *exchange stares.*

105. Interior. Subway station. Day.
LANCE looks up from his paper as the train pulls into the station.

106. Interior. Apartment building. Hallway. Evening.
LISA descends a staircase and knocks on LANCE's door.

                              LISA
                  Lance?

LANCE *doesn't respond.*

                              LISA
                  How are you feeling? ... I heard you
                  were sick.

LANCE *doesn't respond.*

Screenplay

LISA

I was just about to watch one of your
movies. I was wondering if you
wanted to drop by.

LANCE *doesn't respond.*

LISA

I know you don't think they're anything special.... But I do.

Pause.

LISA

Lance, something terrible happened
to me today. I could have saved someone's life. But I ignored them instead.
Has that ever happened to you?
Lance?

107. Interior. Mausoleum. Day.

CLARA *is sitting on the bench in front of the monitor, which plays back an image of* CLARENCE. *It begins as the same video sequence she watched earlier, but then* CLARA *appears in it with a video camera in her hands. She and* CLARENCE *smile at each other. The camera pulls back to show* CLARA *watching this video sequence.*

108. Interior. Apartment building. Lisa's apartment. Evening.

LISA *is watching a scene on her television. In this scene, two people are talking to each other at a booth in a crowded diner. The sound has been turned off, so the dialogue between these two people can't be heard. Behind the head of one of these people, some extras can be seen in another booth. They are out of focus. The camera slowly zooms past the head that figures prominently in the video frame, and onto this group of extras. One of the extras turns to face the camera as he suddenly comes into focus. This figure is* LANCE. *He smiles at* LISA.

109. Interior. Hotel. Conference room. Evening.

LANCE *is having a tele-conference with* CLARA. *He has just described the change in the script to her.*

CLARA

That's impossible.

LANCE

It's true. I could read it to you …

CLARA

You donate your lung to your brother?

LANCE

Yes.

CLARA

But that's not what happened.

LANCE

I know.

CLARA

Did you ask him why?

LANCE

I … didn't have a chance.

CLARA

So what happens to the sister?

LANCE

She's not in the script.

CLARA

They cut me out.

CLARA *laughs hysterically at this idea, fighting back a breakdown.*

CLARA

Did you ask him why?

su.1

VIDEO. IMAGE
OF CLARA
MOVE INTO
HER EYES

su 2

Video image
OF Canœ,
& Clara's
P.O.V.

su 3

FILM
C.U OF
CLARA.

su 4

FILM CU
OF LANCE

Matching singles.

su 5

LANCE

Why can't you?

CLARA

I'm about to be fired.

Pause. She laughs again.

CLARA

Look, you have to tell him that you
need a sister. I mean, the part only
makes sense if you have a sister, if you
donate your lung to your …

Pause. CLARA *realizes the folly of what she's suggesting.*

LANCE

Hmm …

CLARA

You have to do something.

LANCE

I will. *(beat)* Look, it's going to be
difficult to keep coming here to see
you.

CLARA

You have my phone number.

LANCE

Yes. I'll call you.

CLARA

Promise?

LANCE

Yes.

Screenplay CLARA *smiles at* LANCE. *The line is cut.* CLARA's *image remains frozen for a moment, then fades away.*

110. Interior. Apartment building. Lisa's apartment. Evening.

LISA *is watching a tape on her television set. Video image of the guest room that the* HOUSEKEEPER's 'friend' committed suicide in. LANCE *and the* HOUSEKEEPER *are having a conversation in this room. A pair of naked legs lies on the floor in the washroom doorway.*

LANCE

You can't ask me not to worry.

HOUSEKEEPER

No. But I can ask you to stay calm.

LANCE

If they do any sort of investigating
they'll know that I was here.

HOUSEKEEPER

Of course you were here. You're the
maid.

LISA

Lance, what's happening?

LANCE *suddenly notices that* LISA *is watching them. He smiles at her.*

LANCE
(to the camera)

We're having a talk.

LISA

About what?

LANCE

I can't tell you.

LISA

Why not?

LANCE
Because she wants to keep it a secret.

LISA *shifts her gaze to the* HOUSEKEEPER. *The* HOUSEKEEPER, *totally oblivious to* LISA*'s 'presence,' continues chatting to* LANCE. *His words are not heard.*

LISA
What's going on? Answer me!

No response.

LANCE
(to camera. Laughs)
She can't hear you, Lisa.

LISA
Can she hear you?

LANCE
Mm–hmm.

LISA
Then ask her.

LANCE *turns back to the* HOUSEKEEPER. *He begins to talk to her. Again, no sound accompanies the movement of lips. The image begins to go blurry.*

LISA
Lance!

The image is less distinct now, but still visible. The sound has been cut, and all that is heard is white noise.

LISA
Lance, do you need any help?

LANCE *nods.*

LISA
How do I get there?

Screenplay

LANCE *beckons* LISA *beside him.*

                                    LISA
            Lance!

The video image turns to snow.

111. Interior. Hotel. Conference room. Day.
The tele-conference room of the hotel. LANCE *and the* PRODUCER *are having a meeting. The* PRODUCER *is thousands of miles away, and appears on the
video screen.* LANCE *sits with the contract in front of him.*

                            PRODUCER
            Can we move the monitor a little to
            the left please. Thanks. Great. Thanks
            very much.

                              LANCE
            Two things.

                            PRODUCER
            Yes?

                              LANCE
            First of all, I want a hotel room for
            the entire length of the shooting.

                            PRODUCER
            Why?

                              LANCE
            I won't be able to concentrate on the
            role if I stay at home.

                            PRODUCER
            Okay. I'll buy that. What's the second
            point?

Pause.

LANCE

I don't think my character should
donate the lung to his brother.

PRODUCER

No?

LANCE

No, I think it was better ... when it
was his sister. Like in the first draft.
And I also don't like the idea of the
TV talk show at the end.

PRODUCER

You don't?

LANCE

No. ... I think it was better the way
it was.

PRODUCER

And why's that?

LANCE

It seemed to be more authentic.

PRODUCER

Mm-hmm. Authentic to what?

LANCE

To the integrity of the story.

PRODUCER

Can you be more specific?

LANCE

I think the author's point is being
cheapened.

A tense pause. The PRODUCER *stares at* LANCE.

Screenplay

> PRODUCER
>
> Do you know who I am?

> LANCE
>
> Yes.

> PRODUCER
>
> Do you have any idea of the sort of background I bring to a project like this?

> LANCE
>
> Yes.

> PRODUCER
>
> You probably used to watch some of my shows when you were a kid. Right?

LANCE *laughs uncomfortably.*

> PRODUCER
>
> Did you watch television when you were a kid?

> LANCE
> *(laughs)*
>
> Yes.

> PRODUCER
>
> Then you used to watch some of my shows.

> LANCE
>
> So what's your point?

> PRODUCER
>
> My 'point' is who the fuck do you think you are?

Screenplay

> LANCE
>
> All I'm suggesting ...

> PRODUCER
>
> You've been talking to Clara, haven't you?

Pause. LANCE *nods. The* PRODUCER *suddenly changes tone, becoming much calmer.*

> PRODUCER
>
> Look, I just want to make sure that we're working with the best script possible. Do you understand?

> LANCE
>
> But it's a personal story ...

> PRODUCER
>
> Of course it is. It's a very personal story, and I respect that. I just want to make sure that it works as a story. That's my job. I'm giving a lot to this show. I'm directing it. I'm even going to act in it. I know it was a traumatic event for Clara — she was close to her brother. A man gives up a lung to save his sister's life. This is an extraordinary event, isn't it?

LANCE *nods.*

> PRODUCER
>
> And he dies as a result. This moves me, Lance. This moves me so much I want to make it into a very fine film. Something I can share with millions of people.

LANCE
Her brother actually died?

PRODUCER
She didn't tell you.

LANCE *shakes his head.*

PRODUCER
Tragic.

Pause.

PRODUCER
Clara's script deals with what she
went through, but that wasn't what
interested me. So I optioned her
story, and made it mine. And a movie
that takes the form of a talk show is
very original, Lance. I'd watch it.
And people have always watched
what I'd like to watch. You have. Ever
since you were a kid. Right?

LANCE *nods.*

PRODUCER
So, are you ready to sign the contract
now, or not?

LANCE *pauses, then nods.*

PRODUCER
Okay, then sign it.

LANCE *and the* PRODUCER *stare at each other.* LANCE *looks at the contract, then signs it.*

PRODUCER
Good. I'll see you on set.

Screenplay

The conference ends. LANCE *sits back, closes his eyes. Video image of an outdoor movie location and an empty director's chair. The* PRODUCER *is seen walking away. As* LANCE *leaves the room, his answering machine message is heard.*

> LANCE
> Hi, Lance isn't in right now. Please leave a message.

112. Interior. Apartment building. Lance's apartment. Evening.

Shot of LANCE*'s answering machine, which sits on a table next to* LISA*'s roses, recording a phonecall.* LANCE *is seen elsewhere, having his hair cut for the film.*

> CLARA
> *(voice-over)*
> Hi. I just watched your audition again today. I'm dying to see you in the film. Lance … why aren't you returning my messages? I have to know what he said. Do you, do you care about me at all? Do you know what I'm going through? Do …

LANCE *stares into the mirror.*

113. Interior. Cloud Nine video store. Evening.

LISA *returns a tape.* EDDY *stares at her.* LISA *stares back at* EDDY. *Her expression is wild and out of joint*

> EDDY
> You haven't been getting enough sleep.

> LISA
> The tape is different.

> EDDY
> What do you mean?

> LISA
> The tape is different!

EDDY

Alright. Calm down. I'll have a look
at it.

LISA

Eddy, I saw things. Things I hadn't
seen before.

EDDY

What? Other meanings?

LISA

Yes.

EDDY

I guess that's normal.

LISA

And other scenes.

EDDY

That's not possible.

Pause. LISA *looks down.*

EDDY

Listen, I think it would be a good
idea if you cooled off these tapes for
awhile. Get some sleep.

LISA
(looking up)
He's suffering, Eddy.

EDDY

Who?

LISA

Lance.

Screenplay

LISA *turns to leave.*

> EDDY
>
> Lisa …

LISA *stops. She slowly turns around.*

> EDDY
> *(shaking his head)*
> Get some sleep.

LISA *walks out of the store.* EDDY *'s eyes follow her.*

114. Interior. Television studio. Early evening.

A large television studio. The PRODUCER *addresses a crowd of extras, recognizable as the same extras that have been seen in all the movies that* LANCE *has appeared in. The extras are positioned as though they are the audience in a TV audience-participation show.*

> PRODUCER
> Now, what I want you to do is pretend that this is a real show. As if it were being broadcast live, and you are actual participants.

115. Interior. Hotel. Hallway. Early evening.

LISA *walks down a hallway of the hotel crowded with other hotel staff.*

116. Interior. Television studio. Early evening.

The television studio. The PRODUCER *continues his introduction to the extras.*

> PRODUCER
> Now, the topic of the show is organ transplants, and this is a life-and-death issue. Obviously, I need the tension level here to be quite high. A number of you sitting in the front rows have been told that you have relatives or children who are in need of donors. And the actors sitting up

here are doctors who specialize in
the type of operations that could save
the lives of your loved ones.

117. Interior. Hotel. Hallway. Evening.

LISA *walks down the hallway — crowded with people coming and going — towards the door of the room to which she delivered the towels. She opens the door to the room and enters.*

118. Interior. Television studio. Evening.

The PRODUCER *approaches* LANCE, *who is sitting in the audience.* LANCE *stands.*

> PRODUCER
> I'd like to take a moment here to introduce Lance. Lance will be playing the brother of David, the man we are watching on the live feed from the hospital. Can we see the live-feed image for a moment?

On a monitor at the front of the studio, a live-feed image from a studio hospital. On a bed lies RONNIE, *recognizable as the groom from the wedding.*

> PRODUCER
> Can you hear me there, Ron? Ron?

RONNIE *looks up, nods and waves.*

119. Interior. Hotel. Guest room. Evening.

LISA *closes the door behind her. The room seems to be in exactly the same state as the night she delivered the towels. She looks around, into the washroom.*

120. Interior. Television studio. Evening.

The television show has begun. The PRODUCER, *who is playing the host of the show, is moving through the studio audience. We can hear his voice as we look at the live-feed image of* RONNIE *in the hospital bed.* RONNIE *is coughing, and breathing with great difficulty. A nurse is helping him. The* PRODUCER *holds a microphone in his hand.*

Screenplay

> PRODUCER
>
> It's obvious that David isn't the only person in this country suffering from this disease, but he is certainly the only one lucky enough to be on national television. And then I suppose the question becomes, 'Who gets on TV to ask for a body organ'? Who decides? Dr. Spencer, is there something you want to say about this?

SPENCER *is one of the actors on the panel.*

> SPENCER
>
> Well, the main problem is getting access to the donors. The public doesn't seem to be aware of the desperate need for organs.

> PRODUCER
>
> Okay. Okay. But let's take the case of David. How often does a lung become available?

> SPENCER
>
> Not too often. That's because in a trauma, such as, say, a car accident, the lung is one of the first things to get damaged.

121. Interior. Hotel. Guest room. Evening.

LISA *is walking around the room. She opens a closet door.*

122. Interior. Television studio. Evening.

The show continues.

> PRODUCER
>
> Let's talk to David's parents. Can we move the camera out into the hallway?

Screenplay *The live-feed hand-held camera that has been fixed on* RONNIE *moves from the hospital room out into the hallway.*

> PRODUCER
> We'll go into the hall and chat there
> for a second.

As the hand-held camera gets settled, the PRODUCER *addresses the studio camera.*

> PRODUCER
> If you've just joined us, David is a
> young man desperately in need of an
> organ transplant.

At this point, the actors playing David's parents and doctor have seated themselves in the hall outside the hospital room. The actor playing the FATHER *is recognizable from the wedding.*

> PRODUCER
> I don't mean to make your lives more
> complicated than they are right now,
> but something extraordinarily —

123. Interior. Mausoleum. Evening.

CLARA *is sitting, bent over, on the bench. A video image plays on the monitor.*

124. Interior. Television studio. Evening.

The PRODUCER *continues.*

> PRODUCER
> — dramatic is happening to you
> today. Can you give us any indica-
> tion — and I know this isn't the best
> time to ask — but what's going
> through your mind?

The FATHER *is speechless.*

125. Interior. Mausoleum. Evening.

CLARA *sitting in the mausoleum.*

126. Interior. Hotel. Guest room. Evening.

LISA *seems to suddenly be aware that she is framed in exactly the same compo-sition that she observed the* HOUSEKEEPER *and* LANCE *in in her video hal-lucination. She turns to face the camera, the eye of her imagination, and begins to move towards it.*

127. Interior. Television studio. Evening.

The FATHER *is still speechless. He removes his glasses. Cut to shot of the* PRODUCER.

128. Interior. Hotel. Guest room. Evening.

LISA *approaches the camera. Her face hovers inches away from the lens.*

129. Interior. Television studio. Evening.

The show continues.

> PRODUCER
> Can we see David again? Would the
> cameraperson there go in the room
> again just one more time?

The hand-held live-feed camera goes back into the room where David, played by RONNIE, *lies in his bed.*

> PRODUCER
> However traumatic this may be, even
> for those of you in the comfort of
> your homes, I want you to meet
> David.

Cut to shots of CLARENCE *on video,* CLARA *in the mausoleum,* RONNIE *in the hospital, the family in the hallway and then* LISA, *who touches the cam-era in the hotel room. Inserts from this montage re-occur throughout the scene.*

> PRODUCER
> David doesn't want any special

attention. He just wants a chance to
have his story told.

LANCE *stands up from his position in the middle of the studio audience.*

> LANCE
> Excuse me.

> PRODUCER
> Yes? Who are you?

> LANCE
> I'm David's brother.

> PRODUCER
> David's brother?

> LANCE
> Yes.

The PRODUCER *turns to the live-feed image of the parents.*

> PRODUCER
> Is this man your son?

The parents are dumbfounded. They manage to nod.

> LANCE
> I want to make a donation.

Cut to video image of CLARENCE. *Back in the studio, a figure stands up in the audience. It is* CLARA. LANCE *turns to face* CLARA. *The film camera zooms onto the image of* CLARA *in the crowd. The effect is exactly the same as when* LISA *sees* LANCE *speaking on her television. The image of* CLARA *has a hallucinatory quality.* CLARA *pulls a gun out of her handbag and points it to her head.*

Rapid montage of images: the nurse by the hospital bed, leaning over LANCE, *coughing;* CLARA *by the hospital bed, leaning over* RONNIE; LISA *by the*

hospital bed, leaning forward to kiss LANCE; CLARA *with* CLARENCE; *and images from the earlier montage.*

In the studio LANCE*'s face is contorted with terror.*

LANCE
(out of character, in anguish)
No!!!

The montage ends with a shot of the viewing area of the video mausoleum. It is empty. The monitor on the wall is blank.

130. Interior. Apartment building. Later that evening.

LISA *climbs the stairs to her apartment. In front of her door, at the far end of the hall, she sees the crumpled body of* LANCE. *She slowly moves towards this figure. As she arrives in front of* LANCE, *he turns to look up at her. He is very shaken.*

LISA *stares at* LANCE. *She opens the door to her apartment, and enters the hallway, leaving the door open. She sits down in a chair.* LANCE *slowly walks into the room.* LISA *does not look at him. He bends down beside* LISA *and touches her shoulder. She touches his hand, then removes it from her shoulder. She is astonished by his presence.* LISA *slowly moves her hand to touch* LANCE*'s face. They kiss.*

❖

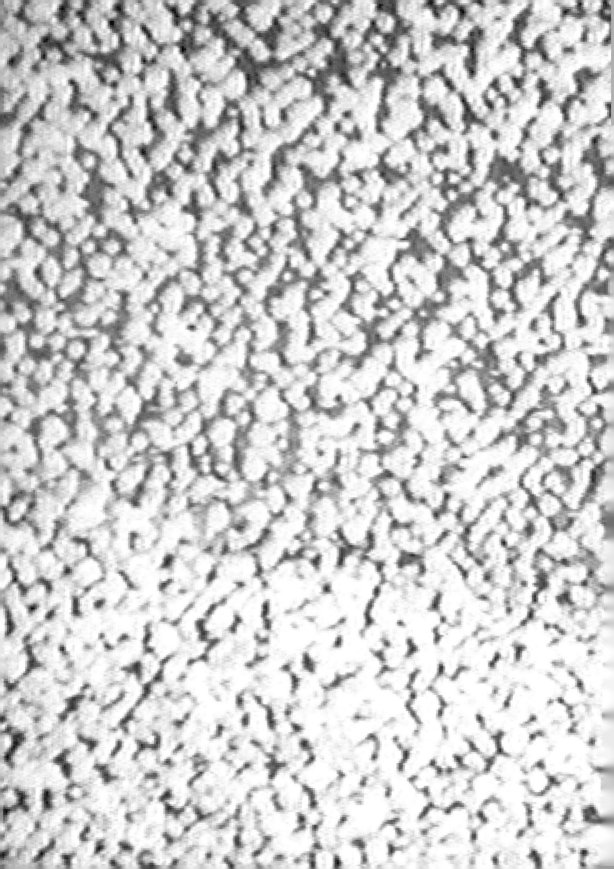

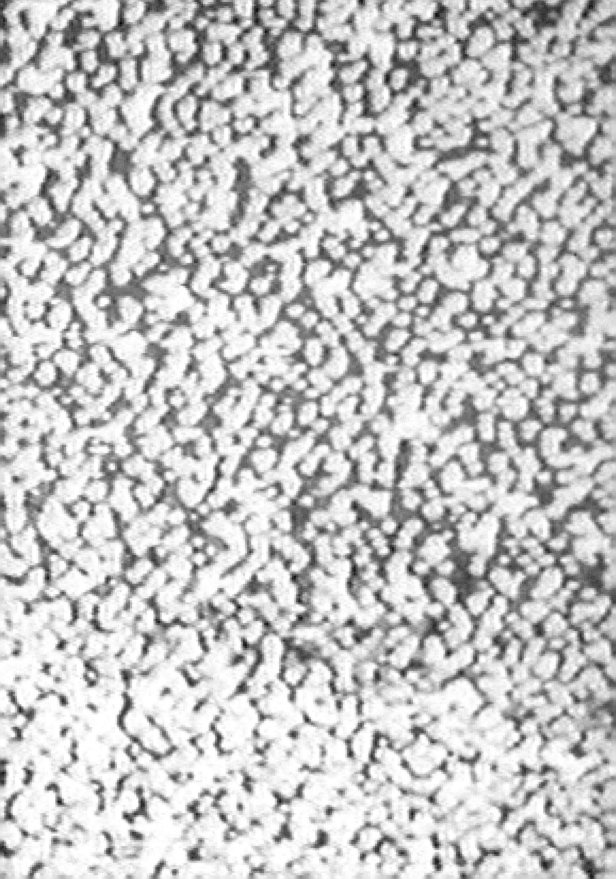

Screenplay *[The scenes which follow, although part of the original script, were never shot.]*

131. Interior. Hotel. Various locations. Day.
*A quick montage of shots, each a glimpse of a particular gesture. No faces are at-
tached to these gestures. Hands sort soiled linen. Hands smooth sheets against a
bed. Used towels are stuffed into a laundry bag. A bathtub is scrubbed. Etc.* ·

132. Interior. Apartment building. Lisa's apartment. Evening.
LISA *and* LANCE *in her apartment, watching the television program that the*
PRODUCER *has made. The show looks exactly as it was seen in the previous shots.*

> SPENCER
> It's very helpful for the patient to vi-
> sualize a donor. It gives them a cer-
> tain optimism and, as well, a sense of
> usefulness.

> PRODUCER
> Does David have a name for this
> donor?

SPENCER *shakes his head.*

> PRODUCER
> Can we see David again? Would the
> cameraperson there go in the room
> again just one more time? However
> traumatic this may be, even for those
> in the comfort of your homes, I'd like
> you to meet David. David doesn't want
> any special attention. He's just like the
> rest of us. He wants to be able to live.

*On the television screen, the image cuts to a shot of a man rising from the audi-
ence. It is the* ACTOR *that has been hired to replace* LANCE. *It is obvious from
the way this man is shot that these inserts have been shot at a different time from
the rest of the show.*

> ACTOR
> Excuse me.

PRODUCER
Yes. Who are you?

ACTOR
I'm David's brother.

PRODUCER
David's brother?

ACTOR
Yes.

The PRODUCER *turns to the parents on the live-feed image.*

PRODUCER
Is this man your son?

The parents nod.

ACTOR
I want to make a donation.

At this point in the original show, CLARA *appeared. But there is no trace of her as the image on the television cuts to a shot of the studio audience applauding. In this shot, taken from the original taping,* LANCE *is spotted in the middle of the crowd of extras.*

LANCE*'s mood suddenly changes as he stares at the shot of the audience applauding. He sees* CLARA. *She is staring back at him.* LISA *turns off the set.*

LISA
It's just the stupid television.

LANCE *is still agitated. He turns to face* LISA. *She moves to comfort him. As she runs her hand over his forehead, he closes his eyes.*

LISA
I turned it off.

Filmography

Howard in Particular

14 minutes, 16mm, black and white

A large company tries to streamline the retirement process by compressing the entire operation into six minutes … without inviting guests to the party. Using an effective juxtaposition of objective and subjective camera angles, *Howard in Particular* examines the strange and obsessive nightmares of one such retiree and his submission to dismissal.

Director, Screenplay, Camera, Editor: Atom Egoyan
Music: Garth Lambert
With: Carman Guild, Anthony Saunders, Arthur Bennett
An Ego Film Arts Production.

After Grad With Dad

25 minutes, 16mm, colour

After Grad With Dad examines the paranoid perceptions of a nervous young man who, upon accidentally arriving at his girlfriend's home half an hour earlier than expected, is forced to maintain a conversation with the girl's father.

Director, Screenplay, Camera, Editor: Atom Egoyan
Music: Garth Lambert
With: Alan Toff, Anthony Saunders, Lynda-Mary Greene
An Ego Film Arts Production.

Filmography

1981 **Peep Show**

7 minutes, 16mm, black and white and colour

Peep Show demonstrates a form of pornography that intrudes upon a customer's more intimate desires. Using an unusual and innovative colour technique, the film manipulates the ordinary into the unexpected, culminating in a peep show in which the viewer becomes the subject of exploitation.

Director, Screenplay, Camera, Editor: Atom Egoyan
Colour Design: Anne McIlroy
Music and Sound Effects: Matthew Poulakakis, David Rokeby
With: John Ball, Claire Letemendia, David Littlejohn
An Ego Film Arts Production.

1982 **Open House**

25 minutes, 16mm, colour

A disturbed real-estate agent tries to sell a dilapidated house to a young couple. It soon becomes apparent that the agent is the son of the people who built the house, and that the entire ritual of selling is a bizarre method of sustaining pride in a household drained of self-respect.

Director, Screenplay, Editor: Atom Egoyan
Cinematography: Peter Mettler
Music: David Rokeby
With: Ross Fraser, Michael Marshall, Sharon Cavanaugh, Hovsep Yeghoyan, Alberta Davidson
An Ego Film Arts Production. Produced with the assistance of the Ontario Arts Council.

1984 **Next of Kin**

72 minutes, 16mm, colour

Catatonically unhappy with his family life, a young man named Peter Foster undergoes video therapy with his parents. One day, while studying tapes at the hospital, he sees the tapes of an Armenian family who feel guilty about surrendering their own son, while still an infant, to a foster home. Peter decides to present himself to this family as their lost son, to finally act out a role different from the one assigned to him in his own life. Filled with haunting images of travel and displacement, *Next of Kin* reveals a young WASP's response to working-class Armenian culture and discourses on the range of roles that life allows us to play.

Director, Screenplay, Editor: Atom Egoyan
Cinematography: Peter Mettler
Production Manager: Camelia Frieberg
Sound Recording: Clark McCarron
Sound Mixer: Daniel Pellerin
Art Director: Ross Nichol
With: Patrick Tierney, Berge Fazlian, Sirvart Fazlian, Arsinée Khanjian
An Ego Film Arts Production. Produced with the assistance of the Ontario Arts Council and the Canada Council.

1985 **Men: A Passion Playground**

7 minutes, 16mm, colour

Perched at the top of a playground apparatus, poet Gail Harris, dressed as a priestess, intones an intensive cataloguing of all types of romantic males. Stretched in a semi-circle below her, men dressed in garb ranging from business suits to track suits give homage to her while chanting 'men, men.' This poetic short is a riposte to the clichés of rock videos.

Director, Concept, Camera, Editor: Atom Egoyan
Poetry and Performance: Gail Harris
Music: Matthew Poulakakis, Perry Domzella
An Ego Film Arts Production.

Filmography 1985 **In This Corner**

60 minutes, 16mm, colour, television

A Toronto boxer, proud of his Irish heritage, is persuaded by the IRA to smuggle a terrorist back to Ireland with his fight crew. Questions of honour and loyalty are in the forefront of this moody thriller, which is punctuated by well-realized fight scenes of documentary-like intensity.

Director: Atom Egoyan
Producer: Alan Burke for the CBC
Teleplay: Paul Gross
Director of Photography: Kenneth Gregg
Editor: Myrtle Virgo
Music: Eric Robertson
With: Robert Wisden, Patrick Tierney, Brenda Bazinet

1987 **The Final Twist**

30 minutes, 16mm, colour, television

Special-effects artists stage an emergency in order to destroy their despicable boss. Working within a typically ironic Hitchcockian tale, Egoyan goes beyond the genre to create a realistic depiction of the workings in a small film-production house. Landau and MacDonald are particularly effective as the womanizing petty film tyrant and the artisan who constructs his 'final twist.'

Director: Atom Egoyan
Producer: John Slan for 'Alfred Hitchcock Presents'
Teleplay: Jim Beaver, from the story by William Bankier
With: Martin Landau, Robert Wisden, Ann-Marie MacDonald

1987 **Family Viewing**

86 minutes, 16mm, colour

This story of mistaken and found identities is set in a nursing home, a condominium and a telephone-sex establishment. Using a collection of video images — television, pornography, home movies and surveillance — the film observes the breakdown and restoration of of a dislocated family. Darkly humorous and unpredictable, *Family Viewing* is a complex journey into a world of brutality and sentiment.

Director, Screenplay, Editor: Atom Egoyan
Director of Photography: Robert MacDonald
Cinematography: Peter Mettler
Production Design: Linda Del Rosario
Production Co-ordinator: Camelia Frieberg
Editor: Bruce McDonald
Script Editor: Allen Bell
Music: Mychael Danna
Sound Design: Steven Munro
Sound Recording: Ross Redfern
Sound Mixer: Daniel Pellerin
With: David Hemblen, Aidan Tierney, Gabrielle Rose, Arsinée Khanjian, Selma Keklikian, Jeanne Sabourin, Rose Sarkisyan, Vasag Baghboudarian
An Ego Film Arts Production. Produced with the participation of the Ontario Film Development Corporation, the Canada Council and the Ontario Arts Council.

1988 **Looking for Nothing**

30 minutes, 16mm, colour, television

Pandemonium strikes an Armenian gathering celebrating multiculturalism when the Provincial Security Force attempts to crack a conspiracy against the visiting premier. This look at contemporary Canadian cultural mores features a set-piece in which security operators are made to dress in ethnic garb in order to infiltrate an official dinner.

Director, Teleplay: Atom Egoyan
Producer: Paul da Silva and Anne O'Brien for 'Inside Stories'/Toronto Talkies
Director of Photography: Andrew Binnington
Editor: Bruce Griffin
With: Aaron Ross Fraser, Damir Andrei, Arsinée Khanjian, Hrant Alianak

Filmography

1989 **Speaking Parts**

92 minutes, 35mm, colour

'I have worked in a hotel for five years. I have worked in film for ten. Both of these professions involve the creation of illusion. In one, the territory of illusion is a room. In the other, it is a screen. People move in and out of rooms. Actors move in and out of screens. *Speaking Parts* explores a terrain that moves between rooms and screens; a terrain of memory and desire. Somewhere in the passage from a room to a screen, a person is transformed into an image. I am fascinated by this crucial moment, and by the contradictions involved in making images of people.' — Atom Egoyan

Director, Executive Producer, Screenplay: Atom Egoyan
Executive Producer: Don Ranvaud
Line Producer: Camelia Frieberg
Assistant Director: David Webb
Director of Photography: Paul Sarossy
Art Director: Linda Del Rosario
Editor: Bruce McDonald
Script Editor: Allen Bell
Music: Mychael Danna
Sound Design: Steven Munro
Sound Recording: John Megill
Sound Mixer: Daniel Pellerin
With: Michael McManus, Arsinée Khanjian, Gabrielle Rose, Tony Nardi, David Hemblen, Patricia Collins, Gerard Parkes, Jacqueline Samuda, Peter Krantz

An Ego Film Arts Production. Produced with the participation of Telefilm Canada, the Ontario Film Development Corporation, Academy Pictures (Rome) and Film Four International (London).

1991 The Adjuster

102 minutes, 35mm, colour, Dolby Stereo

'I have made a film that concerns an insurance adjuster, some film censors, an ex-football player, an aspiring cheerleader, a podiatrist, an actress, a lamp merchant, a butterfly collector and the devoted staff of a large motel. Everyone is doing what they are doing for *a* reason, which is never *the* reason. I wanted to make a film about believable people doing believable things in an unbelievable way.' — Atom Egoyan

The Renders are in the adjustment business. Noah is an insurance adjuster who takes care of the psychological — and physical — needs of his shocked clients. Hera, his wife, is a cultural adjuster: she works at the Provincial Censor Board. When a bizarre couple pays them to vacate their home for a 'film shoot,' the Renders take up residence in the motel that houses Noah's clients and discover just how maladjusted their lives — and those of others — can be.

Director, Screenplay: Atom Egoyan
Co-Producer, Production Manager: Camelia Frieberg
Associate Producer: David Webb
Director of Photography: Paul Sarossy
Production Design: Linda Del Rosario, Richard Paris
Editor: Susan Shipton
Script Editor: Allen Bell
Music: Mychael Danna
Sound Design: Steven Munro
Starring: Elias Koteas, Arsinée Khanjian, Maury Chaykin, Gabrielle Rose, Jennifer Dale, David Hemblen, Rose Sarkisyan, Armen Kokorian
With: Jacqueline Samuda, Gerard Parkes, Patricia Collins, Don McKellar, John Gilbert, Stephen Ouimette, Raoul Trujillo, Tony Nardi, Paul Bettis, Frank Jefferson
An Ego Film Arts Production. Produced with the participation of Telefilm Canada, the Ontario Film Development Corporation and Alliance Communications.

Filmography　　1992　**Montréal vu par ... six variations sur un thème (Montreal Sextet)**

'Episode 4: En passant': 20 minutes, 35mm, colour

A Customs Officer steals one of the luggage tags of a pictogram designer arriving in Montreal, then sketches him and adds the drawing to her collection of 'clients.' The designer sets off from his hotel with an audio tour of Montreal on his Walkman, almost running into the Customs Officer as he wanders through the city. Witty use of pictograms and a sensual response to the environment of a festive Montreal mark this as a gentle, philosophical interlude in *Montréal vu par* and in Egoyan's career.

Producers: Denise Robert, Doris Girard, Yves Rivard
Executive Producers: Michel Houle, Peter Sussman
Directors: Patricia Rozema, Jacques Leduc, Michel Brault, Atom Egoyan, Léa Pool, Denys Arcand
'Episode 4: En passant'
Screenplay: Atom Egoyan
Director of Photography: Eric Cayla
Editor: Susan Shipton
Music: Mychael Danna
Sound: Steven Munro
With: Maury Chaykin, Arsinée Khanjian

1992　**Gross Misconduct**

120 minutes, 16mm, colour, television

The violent life of hockey player Brian 'Spinner' Spencer was marked by drugs, infidelity and murder. Egoyan and scenarist Paul Gross turn this true story into a meditation on the codes of masculinity that delimited Spencer's career and life. Using titles such as 'Trouble in Paradise,' 'What's Bred in the Bone,' and 'Sudden Death Overtime' as chapter headings, they transform a potentially tawdry tale into an essay on the Canadian gothic male.

Director: Atom Egoyan
Producer: Alan Burke for the CBC
Teleplay: Paul Gross, from the book by Martin O'Malley
Director of Photography: Brian Hebb
Editor: Gordon McClellan
Music: Mychael Danna
With: Daniel Kash, Peter MacNeill, Linda Garanson, Doug Hughes, Lenore Zann

1993 Calendar

75 minutes, 16mm, colour

A Toronto photographer invites a different woman to have dinner with him each month. At the end of each meal, the guest makes a phone call to her lover and speaks passionately in a foreign language. The photographer's reveries reveal that his wife has left him for the man who guided their tour through Armenia, where they collected images for a calendar. Wildly humorous and sensual, *Calendar* is Egoyan's most emotionally direct film.

Director, Screenplay, Editor: Atom Egoyan

Co-Producer: Arsinée Khanjian

Director of Photography: Norayr Kasper

Music: Djivan Gasparian, Eve Egoyan, Garo Tchaliguian, Hovhanness Tarpinian

Sound Design: Steven Munro

Sound Mixer: Daniel Pellerin

With: Arsinée Khanjian, Ashot Adamian, Atom Egoyan

An Ego Film Arts Production. Produced with the participation of ZDF German Television and the Armenian National Cinematheque.

Editor for the Press: Marc Glassman
Design: Greg Van Alstyne
Front cover photo: Johnnie Eisen
Back cover photo: John Freeman
Film stills: Atom Egoyan, Johnnie Eisen, Philip
Newton, Tim O'Brien, Fraser Stein
Printed in Canada by Hignell Printing Ltd.

Coach House Press
50 Prince Arthur Avenue, Suite 107
Toronto, Canada
M5R 1B5